Praise for

Love Unend...

"Becky Thompson is the real deal. In he... *Love Unending*, she does not write about lofty theories for building a marriage but rather practical tools that we all can use. I love her honest, down-to-earth style! She writes to those of you who are trying to rekindle the love with which you started your marriage as you're raising children. Even though I don't have young children in my home, I loved the twenty-one-day challenge! This book is for all of us who want to have a passionate, love-filled marriage!"

> —HOLLY WAGNER, pastor of Oasis Church, founder of She
> Rises, and author of *Find Your Brave*

"Too often and too easily I take my husband for granted, and inevitably our marriage suffers, which is why I'm so grateful for Becky's latest book, *Love Unending*. Her words of wisdom and grace equipped me with twenty-one daily (and doable!) ways to be intentional in loving my husband *in light of* how I have first been loved by God in Jesus Christ. I found myself overwhelmed with gratitude for the wonderful qualities in my husband that often go unnoticed. This book was a gift to our marriage."

> —JEANNIE CUNNION, author of *Parenting the Whole-
> hearted Child*

"This book convicted, inspired, and challenged me and had me laughing, all at the same time! Becky beautifully walks us through the real-life issues of marriage that anyone can relate to, while offering a life raft to higher ground. As a wife and mom, I found the daily readings were just the right length for my schedule, and I can honestly say, if you take the time to do the daily challenges, your heart toward your husband and your marriage will be greatly impacted!"

—JENNIFER TOLEDO, pastor of Expression 58 Church, president of the Justice Group, and author of *Children and the Supernatural* and *Eyes That See and Ears That Hear*

"*Love Unending* is a wellspring of life for the weary mom who believes she doesn't have enough energy to keep passion alive in her marriage. Becky articulates the struggles we all face every day as we strive to balance loving our children and husbands well. Sharing personal stories of her own marriage, Becky relates to every mom and wife, encouraging us and challenging us to keep on loving. This book will convict your heart in the deepest way, reminding you of the significance of pursuing an intimate relationship with your husband, despite the demands of motherhood. Whether you have little ones or older kids, you need to read *Love Unending*! I am confident that it will speak to your heart, inspire you, and encourage you in ways you didn't even know you needed! This book is going to radically impact marriages everywhere!"

—JENNIFER SMITH, author of *The Unveiled Wife* and founder of UnveiledWife.com

"The most difficult thing about marriage is the people. When two sinful people enter into one holy covenant, it can be messy. *Love Unending* offers the reader prayerful steps to take toward her husband in a world that constantly pulls families apart. If you're looking for practical marriage encouragement, this is it!"

—KRISTEN WELCH, best-selling author of *Raising Grateful Kids in an Entitled World*

"The first time I met Becky, I knew her books would be as real and passionate as she is. She embodies these very qualities you see on the pages of *Love Unending*. As a mother and also a wife of thirty-six years to my precious husband, I have been challenged by this book to be more intentional about my relationship with my mate. The chapters on listening intently and touching purposefully caused me to dig deep and look at my intentions. Thank you, Becky, for this gift of love to the body of Christ."

—CYNDY MOORING, copastor of Celebration of Life Church, Baytown, Texas

"In *Love Unending* Becky answers the very real question so many women wrestle with: How do I balance motherhood and marriage well? With grace, humility, and hope, Becky uses very personal examples to guide us to the answer, which is, of course, always found in Christ. In this book we have the opportunity to learn how to fall in love all over again each new day, as each new day builds our forever."

—LAUREN CASPER, author of *It's Okay About It*

"If you are a busy mom struggling to keep your marriage a priority, this twenty-one-day journey is for you! With transparency and encouragement, Becky shares the struggles moms face to keep their marriages strong in the midst of motherhood and shows how making one simple decision can impact your marriage today."

—RUTH SCHWENK, founder of TheBetterMom.com and
coauthor of *For Better or For Kids* and *Pressing Pause*

"When you are up to your eyeballs in diapers and dishes, in homework and housework, sometimes you forget to peer over the piles and notice that man you married—the one quietly standing there, blending unassumingly into the background. *Love Unending* will take you on a deliberate twenty-one-day stroll back down memory lane. There you'll discover anew the love you once felt for your husband loooooong before the first kiddo stepped onto your household terrain. This inspiring book—part memoir and part personal journal, tied neatly with a big bow of biblical encouragement—will guide you gently as you endeavor to become the believer, wife, and mother God desires you to be."

—KAREN EHMAN, Proverbs 31 Ministries speaker and *New York Times* best-selling author of *Keep It Shut: What to Say, How to Say It, and When to Say Nothing at All* and *Listen, Love, Repeat: Other-Centered Living in a Self-Centered World*

BECKY THOMPSON

OF SCISSORTAIL SILK

LOVE
Unending

REDISCOVERING YOUR MARRIAGE
IN THE MIDST OF MOTHERHOOD

WATERBROOK

Love Unending

This book is not intended to replace the advice of a professional marriage counselor. The author and publisher specifically disclaim liability, loss, or risk, personal or otherwise, which is incurred as a consequence, directly or indirectly, of the use or application of any of the contents of this book.

All Scripture quotations, unless otherwise indicated, are taken from the Holy Bible, New Living Translation, copyright © 1996, 2004, 2007, 2013, 2015 by Tyndale House Foundation. Used by permission of Tyndale House Publishers Inc., Carol Stream, Illinois 60188. All rights reserved. Scripture quotations marked (ESV) are taken from ESV® Bible (the Holy Bible, English Standard Version®), copyright © 2001 by Crossway, a publishing ministry of Good News Publishers. Used by permission. All rights reserved. Scripture quotations marked (NASB) are taken from the New American Standard Bible®. Copyright © 1960, 1962, 1963, 1968, 1971, 1972, 1973, 1975, 1977, 1995 by the Lockman Foundation. Used by permission. (www.Lockman.org). Scriptures quotations marked (NIV) are taken from the Holy Bible, New International Version®, NIV®. Copyright © 1973, 1978, 1984, 2011 by Biblica Inc.® Used by permission. All rights reserved worldwide.

Trade Paperback ISBN 978-1-60142-810-3
eBook ISBN 978-1-60142-811-0

Copyright © 2017 by Rebecca F. Thompson

Cover design by Rebecca F. Thompson

All rights reserved. No part of this book may be reproduced or transmitted in any form or by any means, electronic or mechanical, including photocopying and recording, or by any information storage and retrieval system, without permission in writing from the publisher.

Published in the United States by WaterBrook, an imprint of the Crown Publishing Group, a division of Penguin Random House LLC, New York.

WATERBROOK® and its deer colophon are registered trademarks of Penguin Random House LLC.

Library of Congress Cataloging-in-Publication Data
Names: Thompson, Becky, (Rebecca F.) author.
Title: Love unending : rediscovering your marriage in the midst of motherhood / Becky Thompson.
Description: First Edition. | Colorado Springs, Colorado : WaterBrook, 2017.
Identifiers: LCCN 2016033857 (print) | LCCN 2016038860 (ebook) | ISBN 9781601428103 (pbk.) | ISBN 9781601428110 (electronic)
Subjects: LCSH: Mothers—Religious life. | Motherhood—Religious aspects—Christianity. | Wives—Religious life. | Marriage—Religious aspects—Christianity.
Classification: LCC BV4529.18 .T4665 2017 (print) | LCC BV4529.18 (ebook) | DDC 248.8/431—dc23
LC record available at https://lccn.loc.gov/2016033857

Printed in the United States of America
2018

10 9 8 7 6 5 4 3 2

SPECIAL SALES
Most WaterBrook books are available at special quantity discounts when purchased in bulk by corporations, organizations, and special-interest groups. Custom imprinting or excerpting can also be done to fit special needs. For information, please e-mail specialmarketscms@penguinrandomhouse.com or call 1-800-603-7051.

For my husband, Jared.
A long time ago, I promised
to love you with all that I am
and all I ever will be. This is my journey
to live out those words every single day.

And for our children, Kolton, Kadence, and Jaxton.
May you always know that your home is built
on Love unending.

Contents

Contents

Introduction

The Secret of Love Unending

*I*f you were eight months pregnant, you probably wouldn't consider it a blessing to live an hour and a half away from the hospital where you would need to deliver your baby. But I did, because that's what brought me to my parents' house that night— the night I found out my dad's secret.

My parents live about fifteen minutes from the hospital where I would be delivering my third child, Jaxton. The hospital has a neonatal intensive care unit, and due to some personal risk factors, we knew a NICU stay might be likely. I didn't want to go into labor and have to make the long drive to the hospital. I need to mention that I live in the middle of northwest Oklahoma, and there are mostly fields and two-lane roads between my house and Oklahoma City. I had this fear that I would deliver my baby in the middle of nowhere next to a wheat field with an audience of grazing cows nearby. So it seemed like a good idea to take my other two

1

children—Kolton, who was four, and Kadence, who was three—
and stay with my parents as my due date got closer. My husband,
Jared, had to stay home and work, but he was prepared to come
running the minute I called and said it was time.

My dad and I were the only two people in the living room that
night. It was about nine thirty, and my mom was putting my two
little kids to bed in her guest room. As I sat there with my dad, I
couldn't help but reflect on everything that had led to that moment.

It had been an exhausting eight months. I had not only been
growing a baby and taking care of my family. I had been growing
an online women's ministry, through all forms of social media, with
a million monthly readers and forty thousand followers across the
globe. I had been keeping up with thousands of e-mails and messages while also trying to keep up with two busy preschoolers. Every
area of my life had felt overwhelming some days.

I hadn't planned to take on the enormous responsibility of caring for the hearts of so many women online, but God wasn't surprised. He knew exactly what would happen when I sat down at my
computer eight months earlier. I thought I was writing a simple
letter on my blog to other overwhelmed women struggling to balance the responsibilities of being a wife and a mom. But God knew
I would wake up the next morning to find that my post had been
shared around the world, forever changing lives (my own included).
He knew my online readership would go from a thousand followers
to forty thousand in just a few months. He knew that nearly ten

million people would read those words and say, "I feel the same way." And God knew what they would need next. He knew they would need to know my dad's secret.

I had received countless messages from women saying, "Yes, I struggle to be both wife and mom. But what do I do about it? How do I balance both? How do I remember to be a wife when it takes all I've got to be a momma?" I wanted to give them a simple answer. I wanted to provide a solution that would change their marriages and restore their hope. But I didn't have it. I didn't know what to tell them, because I was struggling myself to figure out how to keep the love in my marriage fresh. But as I looked over at my dad that night, I thought maybe, just maybe, he could tell me what to do next.

My dad is one of the most patient men I know. Actually, he is *the* most patient man I know. I have never heard him raise his voice to anyone, including my mom and my sister and me. He forgives quickly. He loves deeply. And he is always rational and purposeful with his words. Most of what I know about God and His love for me, I learned from and experienced through my relationship with my dad.

This is why I knew I could trust my dad's advice about marriage. It is because of the way he has treated my mom for nearly forty years. I can't think of a single time my dad was angry with my mom for more than a few moments, and I can't think of a single time he was mean. He has always been a wonderful example of a godly husband and father, and I have always been able to go to him for advice about anything. I remember sitting in the living room looking at him that night and saying, "Dad, what do I tell them? How do I help these women rediscover their marriages in the middle of everything else? How do I help them fall back in love? What do I say to the women who feel as if too much time has passed, who fear it is too late?"

He and I knew that my desperation to find an answer was about more than my pregnancy hormones. It was about saving marriages and healing broken families. It was about giving honest advice to husbands and wives before many even realized they needed help. It was about helping women just like me turn toward their husbands when they feel that so many other things are pulling them away.

What my dad said next changed my life. Sitting across from me in his wingback chair with a late-night cup of coffee in his hands and with the only light coming from the lamp over his shoulder, he leaned in as if to tell me a secret.

"Becky, just tell them to do what I do," he whispered.

I was curious. What secret had my dad been keeping for the last thirty-seven years?! What was his trick to keeping love and joy and peace in his heart all the days of his married life? *What do you do, Dad?* I thought, but he continued before I had the chance to ask.

He looked over his shoulder to make sure my momma wasn't coming, and with a twinkle in his eye and a sly little smile, he whispered, "Every day when I wake up, I tell myself it is the first day I am married to your mom."

He waited for me to catch the truth behind his words, and he flashed a grin when he saw the light bulb come on for me. He nodded. It was as if he knew I was beginning to understand how powerful it would be to live that way. How transformative. How revolutionary.

"Becky, if every day I wake up and tell myself that it is the day I married your mom, then it changes everything. She is just my bride. She is the woman I fell for, and she doesn't have to prove a thing to earn my love. It's a new start every day. There isn't a yesterday full of hurt or offense. There isn't a need for forgiveness. There isn't anything I need to overlook. There isn't a list of things I'm 'counting' against her. There isn't a chance for space to separate us or for us to feel as if we are an old married couple. It's just new love every day."

And there it was. My dad's secret.

The love that my dad shows my momma is an endless sort of love. A love that doesn't seem manufactured. It is limitless, but I had never understood it. I had never understood how he could love so effortlessly, forgive so easily, and live so joyfully. But the reason was right there in front of me—spoken out loud for the very first time. For the last thirty-seven years, my dad has daily made the decision to live as if he were a newlywed—and that attitude has made all the difference.

That night I sat up for a long time after everyone else had gone to bed. I couldn't stop thinking about my dad's words and my relationship with my husband. For so long I had been busy with everyone and everything else. I had needed help with our kids, but I had wanted it my way and on more than one occasion had resolved to do things myself to get them done "right." I had pushed Jared away without realizing it, and as he withdrew further, I was frustrated that he didn't seem to love me the way he used to. I was mad about little things that seemed to build up into much bigger things. I was hurt by little ways my husband made me feel as though he didn't value my work or my time. And I was tired. I didn't know how I was ever going to give any more of myself when I felt as though I was already giving everything I had.

To be honest, I wasn't sure we could ever again experience what we had when we first fell in love: that newness of what it meant to be fully caught up in each other. I wasn't sure I could be the best wife when I was so busy trying to be the best mom. On top of it all, as I thought about my dad's advice, I realized I had been waiting for Jared to love me first. I had been waiting for him to be affectionate or compassionate or considerate so I could respond. I had asked myself over and over, "Why doesn't he just . . ." I kept thinking how I wanted Jared to change.

The answer my dad had given me for the women who read my blog ended up being what I needed to hear the most. My dad's advice was for me just as much as it was for anyone else. But I wasn't sure I wanted to love my husband as I did on the day we married. On our way home from the ceremony, I think we argued about where we were going to stop for gas. For me, the time when love came easiest was long before marriage. Love came easiest in the very beginning of our relationship. I suppose that is why they call it falling in love. It doesn't take much effort.

If I wanted to challenge myself to love my husband the way my dad loves my mom, I had to go back to the beginning—the very beginning. I had to go back before kids, back before marriage, back to those early days when it all began.

Truly, time and children have a way of changing every area of our married lives. But what if we could rekindle that fresh sort of love? What if we could love our husbands first? What if we could change the climate of our marriages by treating each day as though it were the first day we fell in love? We might not be able to go back to the beginning, and we might not even want to. The lessons we have learned in the time that has passed are invaluable. But what if we could couple the lessons we've learned in our married lives with the acts of love that came so effortlessly in our early days of courtship? What if my dad's secret is just what we desperately need?

For the next twenty-one days, you and I are going to remember how we felt and what we did when we first fell in love with our husbands. Armed with my dad's advice and my own experiment of living out his words, I will guide us step by step as we realize that walking in love can be far more beautiful than falling in love.

Each day we will discuss one area of marriage that has likely changed since our first days of being in love. We are going to examine some of the thought processes and behaviors of those early days and see how to continue them now that we are moms. We will cover topics such as speaking kindly, connecting intentionally, and forgiving quickly. There may be days when you think, *We are doing so well with this already!* Celebrate these days! Keep being intentional in these areas as you recognize the importance of connecting in these aspects of marriage. On the other hand, there may be a few days when you think, *Wow. I didn't even realize I felt this way. I needed this reminder.* While the topic for a particular day might not fit your situation perfectly, each one has been designed to remind you of a specific area that has the potential to be better today. Each day is a chance to change your perspective and love your husband intentionally.

As I completed this process, I confess there were days I did not want to try anymore. I was tired. I was still consumed with everything else required of me, and the last thing I wanted to do was remember how great things used to be—or celebrate a husband who I felt was the problem that day. On those days I remembered that this process is about more than just reflecting, because anyone can look back. It is about refocusing our intentions and moving forward.

At the end of each daily read, you will be challenged to walk deeper and deeper into love with your husband. I will ask you to make a few predictions about how you think the day will go or to respond to a few questions. Then we will pray together and prepare our hearts for the challenge ahead. As you complete each day, I hope you will return to the chapter and use the prepared space to journal some of your thoughts and reflections, documenting your progress along the way. As you move from day one to day twenty-one, you have the chance to document exactly what God does through this process. I sincerely believe you will be glad you did!

Friend, there are many routes we can take into our future, but if we want to experience a love unending, we might just have to go back to the beginning. We may have to start fresh daily as we wipe the slate clean and treat our husbands as though it were the first day we fell in love . . . for the next twenty-one days. And perhaps when we have finished this journey together, we will fully understand the secret to rediscovering marriage in the midst of motherhood.

Day 1

Greet Lovingly

Greet one another with a holy kiss.

2 Corinthians 13:12, NASB

How did you meet your husband? Maybe through mutual friends? Or in school? Perhaps it was in the middle of a crowded bar.

Jared and I met at the mall. Now, before you imagine some cheesy exchange of telephone numbers in the middle of the food court, let me clarify. We actually swapped digits inside a shoe store. So, clearly much more romantic.

At the end of my freshman year of college, I took a job working at one of those freestanding kiosks that sell clothes shipped in from Los Angeles, and Jared worked at the shoe store right next to my cart. Every day I went to work hoping that he was working too. I wanted to get to know him more because, well, *he was so handsome!*

Do you remember how you felt in the beginning of your relationship with your husband? Do you remember how much you wanted to spend time with him? How much you looked forward to being together?

Jared and I loved spending time together so much that six months after we first said hello, I answered yes when he asked me to marry him. We wanted to spend all our time together . . . forever.

Now, ten years into forever, I find it easy to forget how much I adored that sweet guy in the beginning. Time has a way of fading those first moments. What about you? Take a second and look back. Can you recall those memories and those feelings? Can you remember how much you looked forward to seeing him after you had been apart?

Every day we overlook so many opportunities to show our husbands that we love them. We don't do this intentionally. We are simply preoccupied with everything else going on around us. Greeting each other is often one of those missed opportunities. How did you greet your husband when you first fell in love with him? If he came over to pick you up for a date or just to spend time with you, did you get up to meet him? Or did you keep doing whatever else you were doing?

My guess is you didn't ignore him. In fact, you probably hugged him. You might have even kissed him. But whatever you did, he likely never doubted that you were happy to be with him again, even if you didn't say those exact words.

As time goes on, the excitement wears off. Some days we are so caught up in our routines that when we do look forward to seeing our husbands come home at the end of the day, it is because we are more interested in their help than their hearts.

I realized this a few years ago when Jared was late getting home from work one day. I should explain first that not only does my husband have a job that often requires him to put in extra hours or to work out of town, but he also is the mayor of our small town and a volunteer firefighter. In addition, he is the media coordinator at our church, overseeing the lights and sound and everything else that ensures our service is broadcast online. Let's just say he gets home late many nights—if he gets home at all. I don't remember what caused him to be late this particular night, but I know I had spent all day taking care of a sick baby and a clingy toddler. It was one of those "Let's see if I can make dinner with one arm and a baby on my hip" kind of nights. The house was a disaster, I had a million things I needed to get done, and I was exhausted. My patience was running thin, and, really, I was just *done*. Have you ever had a day like that? Maybe after a difficult day at work, you just wanted to rest when you came home. Or maybe it was one of those days at home when you desperately needed a break.

I knew that Jared likely had a long day too, but, truthfully, his level of fatigue was the least of my concerns. I just wanted him to come home so I could tag out for a minute and not be in charge of everything in my world. I planned to hand the baby to him as soon as he walked in the door so I could do something crazy for myself . . . like make dinner with two hands. I watched the clock for hours that night, desperate for it to finally indicate that help would walk in the door any minute. As the time got later, I started looking out the window, hoping to see his truck turn onto our street.

The funny thing is, I used to look out the window for his truck when we were dating too. I just looked with a different sort of expectation. I was eager to see him, to spend time with him, to hold him, to be near him. I was looking for *him*. Now I feel as if I am mostly looking for his help.

I wonder if this is ever true for you too. Has the way you look for your husband changed? I think our husbands sense the shift in how we look for them and, consequently, in how we greet them.

Most of us have the opportunity to greet our husbands at least once a day. Some of us stay at home, and others of us head out the door to work before our husbands are even awake. Some husbands come home every night, and others work out of town, work the night shift, or are deployed overseas. But no matter our circumstances, at some point we all get a chance to greet our husbands after we have been apart.

Growing up, I watched my dad come in the front door at the end of his day and walk straight to my mom, put his hand on the small of her back, and give her a kiss. If my sister and I ran out onto the driveway to greet him at his car or hugged him as he walked through the door, Dad would always hug us and then head directly for my mom. He didn't sit down or change out of his work clothes or check the mail before saying hello. Mom came first, and she still does.

I want you to think of the last time you greeted your husband. Did you race to the door and greet him with a kiss? Did you let the kids get to him first while you stayed back changing a diaper or cooking dinner? Did you shout from the other room, "Hey! Glad you're home! Can you help me start bath time?" Or perhaps your husband gets home before you, and you are the one walking in the door at the end of a long day. How did you say hello when you saw your husband for the first time today? Now, how does that compare to the way you greeted him when you first fell in love?

How we greet our husbands can set the tone for how we will interact the rest of our day or evening together. Letting your husband know you are happy to see him—not just ready for his help—is the perfect way to start experiencing love unending.

Today's Challenge

The next time you have the opportunity to greet your husband, do what you would have done when you first fell in love with him. Maybe that means walking away from cooking dinner to meet him at the door and give him a hug. Maybe it means waking up and telling him that you love him and missed him while he was away. Or maybe it means getting to the door before the kids so you can

15

be the first to welcome him home. Think of the anticipation you used to feel when you knew you were going to spend time with him, and then use that memory to show your husband just how happy you are to still be with him today. If your husband works out of town or you won't see him today, consider how you answered his phone calls when you first fell in love. Answer the phone as you would have then. Sometimes we have to remind our hearts how we used to feel so we can get out of our routines and reignite the romance.

Take a few minutes to predict how your husband will respond when you greet him. Do you think he will be suspicious? Enthusiastic? Or do you think he will even notice your efforts?

I think my husband will . . .

_____

_____

_____

_____

_____

_____

TALKING TO THE FATHER

Lord, thank You for being a God who rises to greet me. Thank You for not turning Your back on me but always being eager to spend time with me. Help me remember to show the same kind of love to my husband. Help me show him that I value his heart and not just his hands. Help me show him that he is wanted and welcome. Above all, Lord, fan the flame of love in my heart so I can live fully in the promise that Your love for us and through us is everlasting.

Thank You in advance for the grace to begin this journey of loving my husband as if it were the first day we fell in love. I know You will be faithful to help me in this journey and to transform my heart as I commit to walking in love with my husband daily. I acknowledge that I can't do any of this without You, and I thank You for caring about my marriage and promising You are with me. I love You, Lord, and I commit this process to You. May You be glorified through it all. In Jesus's name I pray. Amen.

Reflect

Describe what happened when you saw your husband. Did it feel awkward? It might take a few days for this interaction to feel normal, but that is why we will repeat this challenge daily for the remainder of our journey. Every time we greet our husbands, we have an opportunity to let them know they are wanted and welcome. Let's take advantage of that daily.

When I saw my husband . . .

_____

_____

_____

_____

_____

_____

_____

_____

Here is how my heart feels today . . .

Day 2

Speak Kindly

A gentle answer turns away wrath,
but a harsh word stirs up anger.

— Proverbs 15:1, NIV

*W*ill you just bring me a towel already?!"
My three-year-old little girl was in the bath, and I was ready to get her out. I had spent a long day at home taking care of three little ones, and all my grace was running out. I was ready to finish giving my kids their baths and put them to bed so I could be off duty.

I dumped one last big cup of warm, clean water down my daughter's back and squeezed the excess out of her hair.

"Jared? Jared? Look. If you're not going to help me with bath time, the very least you can do is bring me a towel when I ask!"

I knew he had heard me. I had heard him open the linen cabinet. To be honest, I wasn't sure there were any clean towels in there. I was behind on laundry (I am forever behind on laundry), and I knew Jared was probably looking in our bathroom or the dryer for a clean towel after finding none where they should be.

"Dig through the pile on the couch! Just bring me anything. Jared? Jared! Are you coming?"

A receiving blanket (you know, those superthin baby blankets) flew into the bathroom and landed on my lap.

"Here. This is the best I can do. There aren't any clean towels."

Of course there aren't, I thought. *I don't have time to do any laundry because I am so busy doing everything else, like giving our kids their baths! If you just helped me every now and then, I might have a chance to wash a towel or two.*

"Can you get Kadence dressed while I give Kolton a bath?" I asked Jared in a tone that was more demanding than questioning.

"Why not? I'm not doing anything else," he replied sarcastically. Truthfully, I didn't care what he had been doing before I asked him to find a towel. Nothing was more important than helping me with our kids so we could put them to bed and be done for the day. At least, nothing was more important to me.

I know this might not be a familiar scene at your house. Perhaps you have never fussed at your husband for not helping you enough. The work load is shared differently in every home. The point isn't what we were doing as much as it is what we were saying to each other and how we were saying it.

Do you remember how you used to talk to your husband when you first fell in love with him? Did you make demands? Did you use a stern tone? Or did you speak kindly? My guess is that you were nice. Patient. Your words reflected the attitude of your heart.

I think back to the first time I had a real conversation with Jared. I used sweet words. I spoke with compassion and consideration. To be honest, I think if I had spoken to Jared on those first few dates the way I sometimes speak to him now, he would have gone running for the hills, and we probably wouldn't be married.

The thing is, with familiarity comes a sense that we can speak more candidly. And we can! Speaking honestly and openly is a part of the trust that we develop over time with our spouses. But honest conversation should never be confused with the permission to be disrespectful. We haven't earned the right to be rude to our husbands just because we said "I do." I think sometimes we speak to our husbands in a way we wouldn't dare speak to another living soul.

Our husbands deserve our respect. Not just because they have earned it, and not just when we feel like giving it. Showing respect says more about the person who demonstrates it than the person who receives it. We respect our husbands not just because of who they are but also because of who we are, and we are women who want to hold ourselves to the highest standard. (And we want to be nice.)

I know it is possible to be married for years and maintain this level of respect toward our spouses because I have seen it firsthand. In my entire life I have never heard my dad say one unkind word to my mom. He's never raised his voice, he's never spoken down to her, and he's never spoken to her disrespectfully. When I look at their relationship and I think about how my dad lives each day as he did in the beginning of his relationship with my mom, I am reminded how the tone of our hearts is reflected in every interaction.

Look, I know it was easier to speak kindly in the beginning, when your busy life or that sweet husband of yours didn't drive you so stinkin' crazy. But I want you to consider your tone today.

I'll start by considering mine. On the night I needed a towel, if I had spoken to my husband the way I did in the beginning of our relationship, I wouldn't have shouted, "Will you just bring me a towel already?!" I might have said something like, "Hey, honey, when you get a second, will you bring me a towel? I need to get Kadence out of the bath." And the way I presented my request would have changed the rest of the conversation. I wouldn't have been frustrated, and he wouldn't have been defensive. The tone of our voices often communicates our hearts more clearly than our words ever do. And we have the power to change the nature of every interaction by speaking with a tone that conveys kindness.

Today's Challenge

The challenge for today might be one of the hardest of all, because it affects every interaction we have with our husbands. But you can absolutely do this. You have children. You do hard things all the time. This will be a breeze. Maybe.

Today whenever your husband speaks to you—no matter what his tone is—consider how you would have responded when you first fell in love, and then respond as you would have in the beginning. But this can't be just one interaction. We are going to begin doing this today and continue it throughout the rest of this journey. It will take practice to remember to speak to our husbands the way we did in the beginning, but it is a discipline worth exercising. It will not only change every interaction we have with our husbands and greatly impact our marriages, but it will also help our children learn to honor and respect their parents and others with their words and tone.

What are your predictions for how your husband will respond?

I think my husband will . . .

_____

_____

_____

_____

_____

_____

_____

_____

_____

_____

What are your predictions for yourself? Is this going to be easy? Is it something you already do well? Or is this something that might take some practice? Write out your thoughts below. They will be fun to look back on when you complete the twenty-one days.

I think this will be . . .

_____

_____

_____

_____

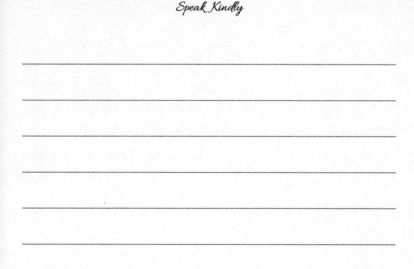

TALKING TO THE FATHER

Lord, thank You for my husband. Thank You for the gift that he is to my life. Lord, I ask now that You would help me remember that You trusted me with my husband's heart when You gave him to me. Your Word says that "a gentle answer turns away wrath, but a harsh word stirs up anger." It is so easy for me to want to snap at my husband and be unkind with my words. But I know this only creates an environment of hostility and discord in my home and in my marriage, and I don't want that, Lord. So I'm asking You to help me give gentle answers and speak kindly in every interaction. Help me remember how I spoke to my husband when I first fell in love with him.

As I consider the gentleness of my tone back then, help me speak just as kindly today. In the name of Jesus, I pray. Amen.

REFLECT

How did it go? Did it make a difference in how you spoke to your husband when you carefully considered each interaction? Were you surprised by the difference? In what ways? What was your husband's response?

Here's how it went . . .

_____

_____

_____

_____

_____

_____

_____

_____

_____

_____

Day 3

Touch Him Purposefully

I found him whom my soul loves;
I held on to him and would not let him go.

Song of Solomon 3:4, NASB

J ared and I had already been on a handful of dates when he asked if I wanted to see a movie after church one Sunday. We had known each other for two months at that point, and we loved spending time together. The entire way to the movie theater we laughed about songs on the radio and what we felt like eating after the show.

Just as we were climbing out of Jared's truck to begin the long walk toward the theater entrance, it started to rain. I'm not talking about just a sprinkle. I'm not talking about a few drops. Without warning, the sky released all it had been holding back, and it began to pour.

I've never asked Jared if he had time to think about what he did next or if it was just a split-second reaction to the rain, but he reached over and took my hand for the very first time, and we ran together through the storm.

I think about that day often and how special I felt when he held my hand and led me to shelter. I'm not exactly sure when I let go. And I don't mean just that night. I don't remember when it stopped feeling special for Jared to take my hand. I wish I could go back and stand on the sidewalk as those two kids ran by so I could shout at them, "Don't ever let go! Hold on to each other forever!"

The truth is, I don't often reach out to touch Jared as I did in the beginning of our relationship. Let's be real. When we first fell in love, we couldn't keep our hands off each other. I kept having to define where the line was. Do you know what I mean? I wanted to touch him all the time. Do you remember feeling that way about your husband? Do you remember the first time you held his hand? The first time you kissed?

No one had to tell you to do those things. In fact, if people told you anything, it was to wait and *not* do it. But after we become moms, so much changes for us concerning touch.

How I touched my husband changed after we had kids because all day long I held babies, nursed babies, and had tiny people climbing on me, pulling at me, and touching me. When my husband came home from work and the kids were finally asleep, the very last thing I wanted was to be touched. I just wanted to lie on my bed or sit on the couch with no one else in my personal space.

This wasn't because I had stopped being attracted to my husband. It wasn't because I didn't want to be intimate with him. It was because being a mom required me to touch and to be touched by my children all day long without having a say in the matter. By the time the opportunity came for Jared to reach out, I wanted to say no to everyone.

Maybe you can relate. Maybe you're in the same place I was. Maybe you would rather have five minutes alone than spend five minutes making out with your husband. Or maybe you are a few years down the road, and your kids are a little older now. But you can remember those early years of parenthood, and you can see the distance they created and how that affects your physical relationship with your husband today.

No matter the state of the physical relationship between you and your husband right now, I would guess that it isn't the same as it was in the beginning. I'm not just talking about sex. I'm talking about simply reaching out for your husband. I'm talking about putting your hand on his back or hugging him just because . . . to remind him that you still see him, to say that you know he is in the room, and to show him that you still love him.

Today's Challenge

The challenge for today is simple, and yet it might be one of the hardest. In addition to greeting your husband as you would have in the beginning of your relationship and continuing to speak kindly, today I would like for you to think back to how you touched your husband when you were first dating. Did you greet him with a hug? Did you send him away with a kiss? Did you reach over and hold his hand while you watched TV? Feel free to take this challenge as far as you feel comfortable. This isn't primarily about sexual intimacy. It is about reconnecting physically throughout the day so that if the opportunity for sexual intimacy presents itself, it won't be the first time you have touched each other all day.

Take a minute to think about your husband. Is touch important to him? Has the way you touch your husband changed since those early days? How do you think your husband will respond?

I think my husband will . . .

_____

_____

_____

_____

TALKING TO THE FATHER

Lord, thank You for being a God who doesn't withhold Your love from me. Thank You for being a God who wanted to connect with me so much that You were willing to become flesh and walk among us. It is in Your presence that I see true love exemplified. You died so I could have a way to touch Your heart. I pray that, just as You continually reach out to me, I will continue to reach out to my husband. There will surely be days in our marriage when we are apart or are unable to touch each other. So while we are able, help us to connect physically. Help me see the moments when I can take the time to hug or kiss him or simply place my hand on his back to let him know that I love him. Lord, help me be an example of healthy touch for our children as they learn about marriage through us. In Jesus's name I pray. Amen.

REFLECT

How did it go? Did touching your husband affect your feelings or your interactions with him? In what ways? How did today's challenge seem to affect your husband? What surprised you the most about your husband's response?

Here's how it went . . .

_____

_____

_____

_____

_____

_____

_____

_____

_____

_____

Did greeting your husband today feel any more natural than it did yesterday? What about speaking kindly to your husband? Update your husband's reaction to both.

My husband's reaction was . . .

_____

_____

_____

_____

_____

_____

_____

_____

_____

_____

By the way, if you feel as if you're not doing the very best job completing these challenges, give yourself a little grace. It's okay!

Write out where your heart is today, and then start again fresh tomorrow.

_____

_____

_____

_____

_____

_____

_____

_____

_____

_____

_____

_____

Day 4

Listen Intently

Everyone should be quick to listen, slow to
speak and slow to become angry.

—James 1:19, NIV

*L*et's talk a little about our hearing. One of my biggest concerns when I became a momma was whether I would hear Kolton if he woke up at night. I am a heavy sleeper. No—scratch that. *I can sleep through anything.* When I was in college, I used to set three alarms and leave notes for my roommate to wake me up in the morning. The semester I didn't have a roommate, I would slip notes under the doors of the other girls who lived on my floor in the dorm, begging them to come and wake me up before they left for class—at ten thirty in the morning. Sleep and I have always been important to each other.

Once, when Jared and I first started dating, he made the two-and-a-half-hour drive from his home in Norman, Oklahoma, to visit me at school in Tulsa. He drove up on a Saturday evening and stayed the night with a friend who lived in town. The plan was for us to drive to my parents' church another hour and a half away the next morning.

Sunday morning came, and Jared arrived in the lobby of my dorm (since no guys were allowed past the front desk) at our agreed-on meeting time, but I wasn't there. He guessed I was running late as usual and called me to see how much longer I would be. But I didn't answer . . . because I was asleep.

The poor guy called me twenty times, and each time my phone rang and rang and eventually went to voice mail. But this is where the story really gets sad. Because school had just started and Jared didn't know any of my friends in the dorm and didn't even know what floor I lived on, he had no way of getting hold of me. So he did the only thing he knew to do. He didn't just sit there. He drove the hour and a half to my parents' church by himself and tried to come up with an excuse for why I wasn't with him.

However, my parents weren't surprised. I am their daughter after all, and they had tried thousands of mornings to wake me from my deepest sleep.

But a funny thing happened the moment I became a mom four years later. Suddenly just the sound of Kolton squirming in his bed could wake me from a dead sleep. It was as if I could hear him while I was still sleeping. But this superhearing power wasn't manifested just at nighttime. It was *all* the time.

And this superpower serves us mommas well. We can be putting laundry away in a back closet and hear a bag of cookies being pulled from the pantry by a not-so-stealthy four-year-old. We can hear the creaking stairs under the feet of an "I just can't sleep" kindergartener and the continued hum of a video game console after we've said, "Enough screen time!"

Our hearing is our secret weapon, but it can also be our greatest hindrance.

Why? Because with the ability to hear everything, we have to learn how to listen selectively. There is constant noise, and although we might have once wondered if we would hear well enough, now we would do absolutely anything for five minutes of not listening to anyone. Have you ever felt that way?

Unfortunately for our husbands, we often tune them out with the kids in those moments where we need mental silence. Our minds constantly play a soundtrack of all the things we have to get done, places we need to be, or things that are weighing heavy on our hearts. And we try to sort through all that while the kids ask a million questions and the TV blares in the background.

So when we are with our husbands at the end of the day, and they tell us about their days, often we don't listen as we should.

Because we have been listening to everyone else all day, sometimes we find it easier to smile and nod than really listen to what they are saying.

I cannot be the only one guilty of nodding my head while chopping carrots and only moderately listening to my husband tell me a story about someone at work being just the worst that day. Sometimes my mind needs quiet like my body needs space, and I push my husband out with everyone else. I just stop listening, as if it's a built-in defense to keep me from becoming completely overwhelmed by all the information for which I am responsible.

But when Jared and I first fell in love, I would hang on every word that boy spoke. I couldn't wait to hear his voice when he called. I didn't reject his calls because I just couldn't handle one more conversation. Instead, we stayed up until all hours of the night sharing story after story and often talking until one of us fell asleep on the phone. When he texted, I responded, and when he spoke to me, I listened. I wanted to hear him. Now I wonder, *Is it even possible to be that way again?*

I've watched my dad model what it means to listen to a spouse. Years ago the newspaper could easily have been his distraction—maybe the Sunday edition or the sports section—but he would put it down and look at my mom when she spoke. Today he mutes the TV or puts down his phone when my mom speaks to him. He listens to her because he cares about what she has to say. And he cares about her.

I know that children change the dynamic of how and when we are able to speak with our husbands. I get it. Sometimes when my husband calls, I'm shouting for my son not to sit on his sister. At other times when Jared tries to tell me something, my mind is in a million different places. I'm thinking about soccer practice or school fund-raisers or that project I just agreed to do but don't really have time for.

But just as choosing to speak kindly to our husbands can change the dynamic of every interaction, choosing to listen fully when our husbands speak carries the same power. It creates a space for our husbands to open up, share their hearts, and know they are fully understood.

Today's Challenge

Today's challenge—in addition to greeting our husbands pleasantly, speaking kindly, and touching them intentionally—is another one that will require us to be very purposeful in how we interact with our husbands. Today we will listen to them. We will choose to really hear them. Every time your husband communicates with you, stop whatever you are doing (if you can) and focus on him. Let him know that you aren't just going through the motions but are receiving his heart and truly participating. This might happen at the dinner table or while you are putting your children to bed. It might happen at the end of your day when the house is quiet and you'd rather rest than invest. Whenever the opportunity presents itself, turn toward your husband.

What are your predictions for how your husband will respond? Do you think he will notice a change?

I think my husband will . . .

_____

_____

_____

_____

_____

_____

_____

_____

TALKING TO THE FATHER

Lord, I pray that You will give me ears to hear. I pray that I would listen better in all areas of my life. I pray that I would hear You more clearly. I pray that I would hear the heart behind what others are saying. And, Lord, I pray that every time my husband speaks, my heart will be drawn to his voice. I pray that I will begin to practice the art of fully hearing him. God, Your Word says that before I speak, You hear, and while I am yet speaking, You answer. You do this because You are focused on me. You see everything that is going on in the world, but You also see the specifics of my life and hear each word I say. Lord, help me not only hear my husband's voice but also listen for the meaning of his heart. I pray that You would bless our communication with each other. And as you do, I recognize that this will not only bring us together, but it will also set a good example for our children. I thank You in advance for all these blessings. In the name of Jesus. Amen.

REFLECT

How did it go? What was the biggest hindrance to listening to your husband? Did you notice a difference when you chose to pay attention? Or have you already been intentional about doing this? How did listening intently to your husband seem to affect him? What do you think could make this challenge difficult to continue? Do you believe it will be worth it?

Here's how it went . . .

_____

_____

_____

_____

_____

_____

_____

_____

_____

Did greeting your husband or reaching out to touch him feel more natural today than yesterday? What about speaking kindly to your husband? Are you noticing a difference in how you relate to each other?

What I'm noticing is . . .

_____

_____

_____

_____

_____

_____

_____

_____

_____

_____

_____

_____

_____

_____

_____

_____

Thank Him Frequently

How beautiful and pleasant you are,

O loved one, with all your delights!

— Song of Solomon 7:6, ESV

When we built our house five years ago, I knew I wanted vaulted ceilings. So many decisions must be made when you build a house, but the height of our ceilings was not something I needed to think about too much. I already had made up my mind, because I have always felt that vaulted ceilings make rooms feel more open and airy. So when the contractor asked if we wanted raised ceilings, vaulted ceilings, or the standard ceilings specified in the plans, I answered easily: vaulted.

However, if I had known then what I know now, I might have answered differently.

The air-return vents in the vaulted ceilings in my living room of course require air filters so dust particles do not clog the heating and air-conditioning unit and cause a fire. Naturally, these filters must be replaced periodically, and with our house located on the edge of a wheat field in windy Oklahoma, the filters must be changed more often than you might think. But here's the thing: the filters are crazy high up (in those vaulted ceilings I really, really wanted), so the only way to reach them is to bring in a large ladder from the garage.

When I decide it is time to change the air filters, I go to the store and buy new ones. I know what I need and how to change them, but my real struggle is that even with the tall ladder, I cannot reach the vent. At five foot two, I'm several inches too short to physically accomplish this task. It's really frustrating that I can't do it by myself.

So I have a solution to this simple problem: I ask my husband to change them. And you might think my supersimple request would have a supersimple answer. But it doesn't. Here is a conversation I had with my husband just last year: "Hey, we really need to change the air filters. I need you to do it because I can't. The new filters are in the laundry room. Will you change them?"

He had just come home from work, and I guess retrieving the ladder from the garage and taking care of it right then was not what he really wanted to do. (Who can blame him?) So he answered, "They don't need to be changed right this minute. I'll do it later."

Unfortunately, "later" didn't come that night. Or that week. Or the next week. So I reminded him: "Hey. The air filters are really gross. Look at all the stuff on the outside of the vent. Will you change them now?" Annoyed that I was asking him once more, he again promised to do it . . . later. I think his exact words were "I said I would change them, and I will."

A month, two months, three months went by, and, to be honest, I stopped asking my husband to change them. I started demanding. "Will you just change the air filters already? I mean, I can call your dad or a handyman to do it if I really need to. I can't do it, and someone else will have to if you won't. The dust could really hurt our unit. Will you just do it, please?"

I felt as if I were butting my head against a wall that wasn't budging.

A chilly Saturday morning a few days later, Jared left for an event with some guys from church, and I decided to turn on our heater. I had just finished having breakfast with our three small children, and I was sitting in the living room with them watching cartoons. I was trying to decide if I wanted to get up and clean not only the breakfast plates but also the dishes from the night before when suddenly the smoke detectors went off. The stench of smoke filled the house as the detectors howled. I grabbed all three of my babies and headed for the front door, calling the fire department on our way out. (I feel this is the perfect time to remind you that my husband is a volunteer firefighter in our town. Oh, the irony.)

I left the front door wide open and parked my oldest two on the porch. Since we couldn't see smoke, I walked back into the house, baby firmly planted on my hip, to see if I could find the source of the emergency. Even though there wasn't any visible smoke, the house smelled like a campfire. I knew the smell had to be coming from somewhere. (Incidentally, while searching for the source, I had to resist the urge to push all the dishes into the sink so my husband's fire brothers wouldn't think we live like pigs.)

Within minutes the fire department showed up (without my husband). They thoroughly searched the house, trying to find the cause of the smoky smell. Looking up, one of the men pointed to the air vents and said, "You should really consider having those changed. That could be what started this whole thing."

I felt so many emotions in that moment. Suddenly I knew exactly what had happened. The air filters were so dirty that they were no longer doing their job, and dust had accumulated on the heating unit. With the vents clogged, fresh air couldn't get into the unit. And in a split second, the dust combusted and sent tiny specks of black soot all over the house, which I was still cleaning up a week later. All because we (Jared) hadn't changed the air filters!

When Jared returned to the house later that day, I didn't need to say anything. He had already received text messages from the guys at the fire station giving him a hard time for missing the fire at his own house. And we all know that the words "I told you so" don't help any situation. The reality was that my husband's decision to keep putting off my request to change the filters created a very serious situation, one that could have ended much worse but thankfully did not.

Obviously, the whole thing could have been prevented. If my husband had just done what I asked, none of this would have happened. But I can't change my husband, and you can't change yours. I feel like that deserves repeating. We cannot change our husbands. So what do we do?

Nagging isn't the answer. Who likes to nag? I don't. Do you? Really, does any wife say to herself, *You know what would be really fun? I would just love to ask my husband to do something over and over again. I would love to feel unheard and unimportant and pushed aside. I would love to get to the point where I'm not just asking, I'm telling, and I'm not just telling, I'm nagging?* Husbands, if you happen to read these words, hear me say, "We do not like to nag you."

I have this theory. Remember in the beginning of your relationship when your husband was so helpful? When you could simply ask him once and he would jump to do anything for you? What was your response? You thanked him. You were sincerely grateful that he had done whatever you had asked him to do. And in addition to being thankful for his doing what you had asked, you noticed and appreciated all the things he did *without* your having to ask . . . because you were paying attention.

So I have a question. Are you still paying attention? When was the last time you thanked your husband? I mean it. When was the last time you considered something he did for you or your family and thanked him for it? If it was recently, awesome! Way to go! But if you're like me, over time we start to take simple things for granted. We start to put expectations on our husbands. *Well, he goes to work, and I stay home with the kids. That's just how it works. Why should I thank him for doing what he does every day?* Or, *He stays home, and I make it possible for us to have this house. What does he do that deserves thanks?* The truth is, sometimes we get so caught up in all the little things our husbands don't do that we forget to be thankful for all the things they truly do for us—all the things we just sort of expect them to do.

Since we agree that we cannot change our husbands, we must look for other ways to change these situations. And I believe, as all the other challenges have reminded us, we are responsible only for ourselves.

We do have a choice when it comes to our actions and inter-actions. We can change the outcome of asking our husbands to do things by examining and altering our own behavior (even if deep down we believe our husbands should alter theirs). We can shift the attitude of our hearts away from nagging by praising our husbands for all the things they do well. This doesn't mean we will have to ask our husbands only once to do certain tasks. But this does mean that perhaps we won't be as frustrated by the things they don't do if we are actively looking for opportunities to praise the things they do. As we saturate our marriages with gratitude and respect, we will create an environment where there is less tension and frustration from unanswered requests.

When you think about it, wouldn't you be more willing to help someone if you felt that the help you had already given that person was appreciated?

TODAY'S CHALLENGE

Today's challenge might require a little bit of effort. If today were the first day you fell in love with your husband, you would probably notice each thing he did for you. You might even brag about those things to your friends and family. Today I want you to thank your husband every chance you get. I have heard my dad thank my mom for doing the laundry, so your husband doesn't have to be tackling a grand task to receive a thank-you. If he is getting ready for work, maybe say something like, "Thank you for all you do to provide for our family. Thank you for all your hard work so our life can be what it is." If he grabs the full trash bag on his way out the front door, don't ignore it; acknowledge it. Praise him for it. And, friend, I really believe that if you look for all the ways you can thank him, it will impact your heart as well.

He might not respond the first time you ask him to do something, but praising him for what he does will show that you don't take him for granted. It will reaffirm in his heart that you are still grateful and that you still notice what he does for you. It will prove you are still paying attention. As you praise him for what he does, you will focus less on the things he doesn't do, and it will help restore the joy you felt in the beginning of your relationship. Before you take on this challenge, spend a few minutes brainstorming the things your husband does that you might thank him for when the opportunity arises.

I need to thank my husband for . . .

_____

_____

_____

_____

_____

_____

_____

_____

TALKING TO THE FATHER

Lord, before I do anything else, I want to thank You. Thank You for the gift of Your Son. Thank You for the life I get to spend with You. Thank You for pouring out Your love on me. Thank You that I get to share that love with others. Because of this attitude of thanksgiving, I experience a sense of joy. I recognize what I already have. When I thank the One who gave me all that I have, it shifts my perspective. Lord, just as it is sometimes difficult to thank You rather than tell You all the things I am burdened by, sometimes it is difficult to purposefully thank my husband. But I know that a thankful heart is medicine for the soul. Help me remain thankful. Help me seek out opportunities to be grateful. Help me remember how I felt in the beginning when I was thankful for this man You have given me. He still is a blessing. Help me treat him like one. In the name of Jesus, I pray. Amen.

REFLECT

What did you thank your husband for today? Were you able to find more than just a few moments worthy of praise? How did this challenge change the way you felt about your spouse today? How did he respond? How do you think continuing this attitude will impact your marriage in the long run?

Here's how it went . . .

_____

_____

_____

_____

_____

_____

_____

_____

Here is how this entire process is going . . .

_____

_____

_____

Day 6

Pray Continually

Pray without ceasing.

— 1 Thessalonians 5:17, ESV

My relationship with Jared began as a friendship. I really had no intention of falling for him. Before that summer we met at the mall, I believed that one day I would marry a man who would become a pastor. I wanted to be in ministry myself, so I hoped to have a husband with a similar passion. Jared had told me in some of our earliest conversations that he was studying to be a police officer. While I believe law enforcement is an honorable calling, it wasn't the ministry I believed my future husband would have. Because of this, I didn't have any romantic intentions toward him. It was just that simple.

I can remember one warm summer night when we met for pizza. Jared had a brand-new motorcycle and asked if I wanted to go for a ride. I could hear my momma's voice in the back of my mind telling me what a dangerous idea it was. But I was eighteen, so I climbed onto the back of that cute boy's bike and held on for dear life.

While we drove up and down the streets of town that night, God asked me to do a funny thing. He said, *Place your right hand on Jared's shoulder and pray for his wife.* And so I did. I prayed that God would bless her. I prayed that the Lord would guide her and protect her. I prayed that God would be with her at that moment. I prayed that she would know Jesus more personally. I prayed that she would know with certainty that Jared was the man for her. And I prayed that God would bless their marriage.

It took nearly six months for me to realize I had prayed for myself that night as we set out on one of our first journeys together. For years I had prayed for my future husband without knowing who he was. Throughout high school and then college, I wrote down my prayers and journaled notes to the man who would one day be mine. I knew that the guy I would eventually marry wouldn't just materialize out of thin air and that at the exact moment I was praying, he was living the days that would become his past. And I knew that the choices he made then would have ripple effects into our marriage. So I prayed that God would guide him. I prayed that the Lord would turn my future husband's heart toward Jesus. I prayed that God would bring people into his life who would help him make good decisions. And I prayed that the Lord would protect him—all before I knew that Jared was that man.

But something happened when Jared and I got married. I'm not proud to admit it, but the truth is, I stopped praying for him the way I used to. I had been so passionate about praying for my future husband before I knew I would marry Jared. But when my husband was sitting across the dinner table from me and wasn't just an idea over the horizon, I stopped passionately asking the Father to intervene on his behalf. I stopped asking God to give him good dreams, to protect his steps, and to guard his heart. I stopped reminding God of His promises for us as a married couple. When that happened, I didn't hurt just Jared. I hurt both of us, because prayer is the most powerful tool we have to change our circumstances. God can change the things that we cannot, and the Word of God says that He listens and answers before we even ask.

Did you ever pray for your husband before you knew him? Were you like me, with journals of thoughts and prayers for him? Once you realized who your husband would be, did you continue to pray with the same fervency? Even if you didn't pray for your husband before you knew him, do you pray for him now? Is setting aside time to talk to God about your husband a high priority? Often it isn't that we don't care, but prayer gets pushed further and further down our list of things to do. That is why today's challenge is so important.

Today's Challenge

Today we are going to begin a prayer routine for our husbands. We are going to take five minutes to pray (maybe while we shower or brush our teeth or find a clean shirt to wear). Did you know God hears the prayers of a busy woman? It is so important to carve out specific time to pray, but if you just cannot—if you don't know where you would find even five minutes at the beginning or end of your day—start by praying while you are doing something else, like washing the dishes.

Maybe you don't know where to begin when it comes to praying for your husband. Maybe praying for him isn't something you have done before or even considered. If that is the case, I'd like to make today's challenge a little easier for you. The Word of God says in Proverbs 4:23, "Above all else, guard your heart, for everything you do flows from it" (NIV). We shouldn't start by praying that just our husbands' actions will change. We shouldn't start by praying that just our husbands' words or even thoughts will change. If we want to see God transform our husbands, we need to start praying for their hearts. For today's challenge, whether or not you have a habit of praying daily for your husband, begin to pray these ten prayers over your husband's heart.

Lord, I pray that my husband's heart will be . . .

1. *confident* of Your love for him,
2. *sensitive* to the promptings of Your Holy Spirit,

3. *brave* as he follows You in all areas of his life,

4. *compassionate* so that he may show Your love to others,

5. *wise* in always discerning truth,

6. *gentle* with my heart and the hearts of our children,

7. *receptive* to my love for him,

8. *strong* in doing what You have called him to do,

9. *protected* from the lusts that would try to ensnare it,

10. *reflective* of the love of his heavenly Father.

What are some of the other things that you are praying for your husband today? While most of the other days prompt you to predict the outcome of the challenge, today let's write out our petitions before the Lord. Write out your own prayer below, and be specific about the things you are asking God to do in your husband's life and in your marriage. Wouldn't it be wonderful to look back someday and see how God answered these prayers?

Dear heavenly Father,

_____

_____

_____

_____

_____

_____

_____

Talking to the Father

Lord, I admit that some days I wish You would just fix my marriage and would start with my husband. There are days when I feel he is the problem, when I wish he realized how much he frustrates me. Maybe if he realized this, he would change and our marriage would get better. But, Lord, sometimes I wonder if he thinks the same things about me. God, the most powerful tool You have given us to improve our marriages is prayer. Help me bring my husband before You daily. God, I want to be a wife who acknowledges that her husband deserves her prayers. He deserves a wife who continually intercedes on his behalf—not so that You will fix him, but so that You will bless him, walk beside him, and know what is most important to his heart. God, no matter what my prayer life was like when my husband and I first fell in love, help me see the purpose and the power in praying now. You are so faithful to answer when we call, and right now I just place my marriage at Your feet. Continue to guide me as I remember what it means to be a praying wife. Help me choose to walk in love always. In the name of Jesus, I pray. Amen.

REFLECT

Were you able to find time to pray for your husband? When? Did praying for your husband change the attitude of your own heart? Describe today's interactions with your husband. How is this process going, friend?

Here is my update . . .

_____

_____

_____

_____

_____

_____

_____

_____

_____

_____

Day 7

Forgive Immediately

Just as the Lord forgave you, so also should you.

— Colossians 3:13, NASB

Jared and I were walking hand in hand into the mall just days into our brand-new relationship. Before I go any further into this story, doesn't that just sound lovely? We weren't wrestling a stroller. We weren't making a game plan for how we could get in and out of the shops with our three kids. We weren't there for one item and one item only. We weren't at the mercy of a ticking clock that would tell us when we needed to pick up our kids from the baby-sitter. We were just there at our leisure. We were walking and shopping and talking and spending time together because we wanted to and because we could. Oh, the things all of us take for granted before we have children.

It was during this blissful trip to the mall that we passed a couple that was not having such a pleasant experience. Actually, they were in the middle of a nasty disagreement. I'm not sure what they were upset about, but the wife was yelling at her husband, and the husband was walking three feet in front of her and refusing to turn around. I'm not big on judging people at all, let alone based on one fleeting moment, but it was obvious to anyone around that they were very upset with each other.

As I rested my head against Jared's arm, I squeezed his hand, looked up into his eyes, and very naively asked, "Do you think we will ever fight like *that*?" I couldn't imagine having a moment with him that wasn't full of absolute bliss. I sincerely believed that no issue would ever outweigh our feelings of love.

Do you remember feeling that way? Do you remember how easy it was to overlook small disagreements or differences of opinion? Because you loved that guy so much, did those little things not seem to matter?

As time goes on, our negative feelings sort of snowball. The things we loved in the beginning might begin to annoy us. The little issues we were able to overlook suddenly don't seem so insignificant. And before we know it, small issues turn into bigger issues, which gain momentum and turn into more and more destructive arguments.

I think there is a simple reason we didn't fight as passionately in the beginning as we might now. In the beginning we didn't carry around a huge list of all the wrongs our husbands had committed. I'm not saying we all do that now. Certainly not on purpose. But in the beginning, if something happened that made us feel a little upset, we either set it aside or addressed it immediately. We didn't bury it or hold it against our guys. We were so much quicker to let it go or overlook it altogether.

So today ask yourself, *Has my husband done anything that has frustrated me? Annoyed me?* Surely I'm not the only one who must painfully admit that I can think of at least three things my husband has done since lunch that aggravated me. The problem is, if I don't forgive him quickly, if I don't address it in my heart and remember that the man who loves me does make mistakes, if I don't release him from the obligation of making that wrong right even before he has a chance to apologize for it, then I have created one of the most dangerous things in my marriage. I will have begun a list.

The Word of God reminds us that love keeps no record of wrongdoing. The reason for this is simple. God knows how destructive unforgiveness truly is. He knows that if we don't forgive and let it go, we will reflect on those moments later whether we want to or not. They become anchors in our hearts that don't drag down only our spouses; they can also cause us to drown.

Here's an example. Let's say Jared chose to take a phone call during dinner instead of sitting down to eat with us and that hurt my heart. If I don't address it with him or forgive him for it immediately and instead choose to be offended and keep that offense to myself, then the next time he does something similar, I might find myself even more frustrated. But Jared won't understand why I am upset the second time if I didn't tell him when it happened the first time.

As a matter of fact, my response to the second event might seem out of proportion because my frustration has built up since I failed to address it appropriately the first time. Has this ever happened to you? You have been upset because your husband *never* does this or *always* does that. And when you finally tell him how upset you are, he feels completely blindsided because you don't have just one moment in front of you. You have a week's (or a year's or an entire marriage's) worth of moments that you haven't let go. Sound familiar?

I know that in the beginning of your relationship the issues you faced as a couple might have been more trivial than the circumstances you deal with now. You might have argued over what movie to see or what you were going to eat for dinner or how you were going to spend your Friday night. Now you may be dealing with parenting and jobs and schedules and deeper heart issues like insecurity or even betrayal.

But we still have to get back to the place where we can forgive our husbands quickly—almost immediately. I'm not talking about sweeping things under the rug. Too often the things we thought we had let go of have actually been pushed down deeper, and we don't realize it until they grow ugly roots.

I'm talking about fully considering each moment when you

have a disagreement with your husband and either setting an appropriate time to discuss it or choosing to fully forgive him and wipe it from your heart and your list.

They say unforgiveness is like drinking poison and expecting the other person to die. Just think about it. How many times have you sighed heavily, given your husband a dirty look, or had a generally bad attitude and hoped he would pick up on the fact you're upset with him? And how many times has he missed every not-so-subtle hint? We are fuming, and they are going about their days without a clue anything is wrong. Choosing to hold on to offense always hurts us more than it hurts the person who has offended us. But when the other person is our spouse, unforgiveness destroys both people. It is a blow to the entire marriage because our hearts are one.

Look, I don't know what has happened between day one and now. I don't know if your spouse has done some things that seem completely unforgivable, and I don't know what lists you have made or what past offenses you are holding on to. But I know that Scripture says we should forgive each other just as the Lord forgave us. Goodness, that sounds like hard work sometimes. But if we really want to move forward, if we want to be whole and find a way to love each other with the same sort of passion we felt in the beginning, then we have to take a deep breath and ask the Lord to help us really forgive our husbands for whatever past hurts we are harboring in our hearts. We have to tear up the lists.

Today's Challenge

Today I would like you to make a list of some things your husband does that drive you crazy. It can be anything: He doesn't take the trash out even though you put the bag by the back door. He doesn't notice or appreciate the small things you do for him. Take your time to really think it through. What are some of the little things that have been bothering you?

My husband drives me crazy when he . . .

_____

_____

_____

_____

_____

_____

_____

_____

_____

_____

Now I want you to ask yourself these questions: Have you addressed these things in an appropriately toned conversation? Have you talked to your husband about each item individually? Or have they built up so that when you address one of them, you use the other items on the list as weapons, attacking the quality of his character?

Now, in a separate list below, write out all the things your husband has done that hurt your heart and that you are still carrying today. I'm not talking about any issue that you feel is resolved. I'm talking about the things that you tried to let go of but haven't been able to. Maybe it was something that happened early in your marriage, or perhaps it is something that happened just this week. Whatever it is, take a minute to write the list below, starting each item in the middle of the line. You will see why in a minute.

I need God to help me forgive my husband for . . .

_____

_____

_____

_____

_____

_____

_____

_____

_____

_____

Now, in front of each item on the list, I want you to write the words "I forgive [insert husband's name] for . . ." And then say each item on the list out loud. Confess with your mouth and believe with your heart, and then truly place each offense into the hands of Jesus, asking Him to help you forgive your husband just as He has forgiven you. Completely. Fully. Forever. One of the first steps in healing any part of marriage is choosing to take a step toward forgiveness. And sometimes that first step looks like addressing the things that have created space between you and your spouse.

Once we address these lists, we will truly be able to live each day as if it were the first day that we fell in love. But we cannot do it on our own. We will need the Lord to continue to teach our hearts how to fully forgive daily.

TALKING TO THE FATHER

Father God, thank You for forgiving my sins. Thank You for removing each of my offenses. Thank You for no longer seeing those things when You look at me but instead seeing a brand-new creation. Lord, right now I give You my list. I place in Your hands the record of hurts and offenses that I have carried for too long. I ask that You would take it and begin to heal those hurts. Help me forgive my husband as You have forgiven me. Completely. Totally. Without holding anything back. God, free my heart from the pain that came from each moment. Heal the wounds created by each offense. God, I'm asking for a miracle. I'm asking for a brand-new start. Help me trust my husband. Help me move past these moments and leave behind every hurt so I am free to love my husband fully. And, Lord, may this be a reference point for the grace You are asking me to give moving forward. Help me to forgive continually, never keeping my pain as a weapon to use later. May each moment of forgiveness be a moment that I move closer to my husband instead of allowing the offense to linger and push us further apart. Thank You, Lord. It is in the name of Jesus that I pray. Amen.

REFLECT

After making your lists and praying, do you feel a change in your heart? If so, write out your experience. As you move forward, how do you think forgiving your husband quickly will impact your marriage?

Here's how things are changing . . .

_____

_____

_____

_____

_____

_____

_____

_____

_____

_____

_____

Day 8

Expect Gracefully

Forgetting the past and looking forward to
what lies ahead, I press on to reach the end of
the race.

Philippians 3:13–14

We were just a few months into our dating relationship the night that Jared got a call from his brother, Josh. It was about nine o'clock, and Jared and I were snuggled up on his couch watching a movie at his apartment. It was just a regular night, but when the phone rang and Jared answered, right away I knew something was wrong. I listened from a few feet away, trying to figure out who had called and what was happening. I was able to make out only a few words: "Kids. Meet me. Hurry." Jared hung up the phone and explained that Josh had an emergency and needed us to watch his kids for a few hours.

I remember thinking, *What are we going to do with them?* To clarify, I didn't have any younger siblings or immediate relatives growing up. I never baby-sat, nor did I help in our church nursery. To be honest, I had never been responsible for anyone but myself— ever. And as a sophomore at a university that had a mandatory curfew and dress code, I hadn't really mastered taking care of myself on my own yet either.

However, Jared had been around young children all his life. He came from a large extended family with lots and lots of babies, and he became an uncle when he was just fourteen. He didn't answer me when I asked in complete exasperation, "Well!? What are we going to do with them?" I am sure he thought I was joking. He drove us to meet his brother and moved the car seats into his vehicle. I just stood there with an exaggerated smile on my face, wondering how we would survive the next couple of hours.

As we loaded up those sleepy-eyed babies and buckled them in tight, I proudly announced, "Well! Are you guys hungry? Let's go to McDonald's!" *Every kid loves McDonald's,* I thought. *I totally just became the world's greatest adult.* Except kids love McDonald's when it isn't an hour past their bedtime and they aren't visiting a strange uncle and almost-aunt that they rarely see.

Twenty minutes later as we sat in the restaurant eating nuggets and fries and drinking something orange, I remember thinking, *I'm nailing this faux-mom thing. This is what success looks like. I'm going to be the best mom ever. I totally have this.*

But I remember thinking something similar about Jared. Seeing him with those overtired babies chowing down on Happy Meals late at night made me think all of these "someday" thoughts.

Did you ever have those? *Someday this man is going to be the very best dad. He is going to be kind and helpful and funny and just the greatest. He's going to be silly and make the kids laugh, and he's going to be a protector and make them feel safe. He's going to be firm but gentle . . . He's just going to be wonderful.*

But let's be real for a second.

Do you know how frustrated I would be with my husband today if he took our kids to get McDonald's late at night when they have school the next day?

Let's just pause and agree that my idea that night was absolutely ridiculous. I mean, who does that? We should have offered to go to Jared's brother's house and sit quietly with his kids so they could sleep in their own beds.

I know better now. We both know better now. As a matter of fact, the biggest difference between that night and today is one thing—experience. Experience has taught us what we couldn't have possibly known then.

The same is true for my relationship with Jared. All those things I felt toward him that night and all those expectations that filled my heart about the type of father he would be "someday" were just as naive as my own parenting ideas.

Neither was based in reality. It would be four years before I would witness Jared in his role as daddy. But if I'm being honest, I'm guilty of not allowing my expectations to grow with my experiences. After ten years of marriage and six years of parenting, I know my husband well. I know how he thinks, how he feels, and how he acts. But while I have watched him grow as a man, for some reason I still try to make him fit the expectations of who I believed he would be—or thought he should be—someday.

It is so much fun to dream about who our husbands will be someday, until someday turns into the present day and we have to reconcile our expectations with our realities.

During this process of reflection, we often go back and consider how we felt or what we did in the early days of the relationship, and we do those things again. We remember how we spoke in the beginning. We work on greeting our spouses as we did in the beginning. We revisit old behaviors as a way to rediscover what used to be. But there are moments like this one when we look back and think, *I felt that way in the beginning, but I need to apply the filter of experience. I need to let go of who I thought my husband would be someday and fully allow him to be the man he is today. I need to go back to how I felt when I gave my husband the grace to be whoever he might become and apply that same grace to the man he is now.* We need to let experience be the filter through which we create new expectations.

Looking back at my parents, I don't think there was ever a time when my dad's expectations put my mom in a box. Whether she went to work or stayed home with us kids, he didn't stop her and say, "That's not who I thought you would be" or "That's not how I thought you would parent." He cheered her on and grew right alongside her.

If we are going to treat our spouses as we did when we first fell in love, we must give them the grace to become whoever they are going to be—outside our expectations and right in the middle of ordinary life.

How would we interact with our husbands if we gave them the grace to continue to become who they are and who they are meant to be?

Today's Challenge

So what is the challenge today? I want you to consider some of the expectations you have of your husband, specifically when it comes to parenting. Do you ever find yourself frustrated that your husband doesn't interact with your children the way you want him to or the way you do? Can I remind us both of something? He will never be you. He will never think or feel or act the way you do.

God made our husbands different from us, and He made them different for a reason. Dads will interact and engage and play differently. They will push and inspire and encourage differently. They will teach and coach and motivate differently. Today's challenge? Let him. Let go of your old or unfair expectations so he can be just who God has called and created him to be. Let's do this by writing down some of our unmet expectations and then in our hearts releasing our husbands from the burden of not being or doing or becoming what we had imagined they would. Have grace for who your husband is—as if it were the first day you fell in love.

Expectations I need to let go of are . . .

_____

_____

_____

_____

_____

_____

_____

_____

_____

_____

_____

Talking to the Father

Lord, You knew exactly what You were doing when You gave me my husband. You knew the man he was at that moment, and You knew the man he would be today. God, so often I want him to be the dad I expected him to be. I want him to do things the way *I want* him to do them. But, God, I'm asking for Your help. Lord, help me give my husband the same freedom I gave him in the beginning, when my heart was wide open to the man he is. Help me continue to let my husband become who You have called him to be without my putting restraints on him—even the restraints of my own expectations. Thank You, Lord, for helping me continue to love my husband well and for reminding me to give him the same grace I crave for myself. In Jesus's name I pray. Amen.

Reflect

How do you foresee this challenge affecting your marriage? Do you think your husband knows that you have these unfulfilled expectations? Have you ever addressed these issues with him? How do you think letting go of them will change the dynamic in your home?

By letting go of these expectations, I think . . .

_____

_____

_____

_____

_____

_____

_____

_____

Now let's talk about how you're doing. What's really going on in your heart right now? How are you feeling about this whole process? What is God showing you?

_____

_____

_____

Day 9

Serve Joyfully

Let's not merely say that we love each other;
let us show the truth by our actions.

1 John 3:18

*I*t was the end of the summer, and that meant it was time for me to move back to Tulsa so I could begin my sophomore year of college. I was absolutely *not* falling in love with Jared. I was just his friend. I was going to marry a pastor, and Jared wanted to become a police officer. I was *not* falling in love with him. *Except I was.* I was crazy about him. And some days I acted a little crazy just to prove it.

One afternoon a few weeks before I had to move, I decided to cook dinner for Jared while he was at work. Since I was just eighteen and my mom still made most of my meals (I wish this weren't true), I decided I would make the only fancy dinner I was sure I couldn't mess up: a precooked rotisserie chicken from the grocery store with a side of bagged salad, a can of corn, and a package of Hawaiian rolls. It was going to be magical.

Since he was at work, I knew I would need help getting into his apartment to set it all up before he returned. So I got in touch with his cousin who lived in the same complex and had a spare key, and I sneaked in. The entire apartment was so small it could fit in our current master bedroom closet. So even though there wasn't much actual cooking going on, preparing the meal was still a challenge.

Jared called me as he left work, and I pretended I was at my own house. He believed me, but I hadn't thought it all through when I planned my surprise. Instead of parking around the corner to hide my car, I parked in front of his building. As he pulled up to his apartment, he knew right away that I was inside. So while he wasn't surprised I was there when he walked in the door, he was genuinely amazed that I cared enough to prepare a meal and do something special for him—even if it wasn't elaborate or unique.

Do you remember doing fun or thoughtful things for your husband when you first fell in love? I'm not talking just about surprising him. Do you remember all the little things you did for him simply because you loved him and it was your joy to do them? I can think of many other moments—like the time I helped him with his laundry, just because. These were simple acts that were a natural response to how I felt about him. I served him joyfully out of the abundance of love I had for him.

Less than a year after that surprise dinner, we were married and eating each meal as husband and wife. In those early days I thought it was so much fun to be responsible for taking care of Jared's needs. Simple things like fixing meals and washing clothes were fun. Yes, I said *fun*. Through these small acts, I could tell Jared in a million little ways throughout the day that he was loved and cared for. Maybe your acts were different from mine, but I'm guessing that whatever you did for your husband in the beginning of your relationship, you did with joy.

Then something happened at our house. Well, three somethings happened. We named them Kolton, Kadence, and Jaxton, and while they are the three sweetest little somethings, they changed this particular dynamic of my relationship with Jared. With the addition of babies came less time and less energy I could give to him. I'm fairly certain this is true in every home. I cannot be the only person who has gone from finding ways to show her husband that she loves him to feeling as if she has four children instead of three and wishing her husband could just take care of himself. Don't get me wrong. My husband doesn't actually need me. He can do all the things that I do for him on his own. But there are days when doing things for him feels like work.

It seems that most days I am waist deep in dirty diapers, homework projects, and children who are fighting while I'm trying to maintain my house and my job and my sanity. On those days I want to look at my husband and say, "Dude, I don't know where your extra socks are. If there aren't any in your drawer, wash some before you need them, and until then you'll have to find a pair yourself. Figure it out. I can't even begin to care about that right now." Then I feel terrible about it. Often I wish that I felt as I did in the beginning when going out of my way to do nice things for him was fun and came naturally. But secretly some days I feel as if my husband is just one more person I have to take care of. Instead of being the helpmate for him that I was created to be, I end up resenting the moments he adds one more thing to my to-do list.

Perhaps there have been moments in your marriage when serving your husband felt more like your job instead of your joy. I think our husbands often feel like this is true even if we never tell them. They know we are already spread thin, and they don't want to feel as if the things we do for them are a burden. I think my husband would confess that he misses the days when my doing thoughtful things for him didn't come with the expectation of reciprocation. When my act of service was a gift, not a trade-off for something he could do for me later.

If I stop to consider my attitude, I wish things were different. I wish I had unlimited time and attention to give to Jared. But more than that, I wish I could operate from a place of overflowing love, as my dad does toward my mom.

Every morning for the last thirty-seven years my dad has brought my mom a cup of tea with a spoonful of sugar. He sets it down next to her with a smile as if it were the very first cup of tea he has ever prepared for her. I've often thought about that simple act and reflected on ways I could show my own husband that same kind of selfless love.

So you might be thinking, *Becky, this is great. I want to perform simple gestures of love for my husband, but I don't have time to do anything more for him. I am already overwhelmed by all that is expected of me. Actually, I need him to help me more. That's what would really help our marriage.* Or maybe you still perform simple gestures of love for your husband, and you're thinking, *I already do as much as I can for him. I try my hardest to show him that I love him. What more do you want me to do?*

Sister, that's the beauty of today's challenge. It might just be the easiest one yet, because I'm not asking you to *do* anything different. Let's stop for a bit and think back on all the things we did for our husbands when we first fell in love. Really pause and remember. Now I want you to compare those feelings with how you feel today. When you throw his socks and underwear into the washing machine, or when you pick up the dry cleaning for him on your way home from work, are you doing it out of obligation because it's one of the responsibilities you take care of? Practically speaking, the answer might be yes. But I want you to think about how you felt the first time you took care of something so simple for him. Each little act felt . . . purposeful. And most of them were sincere acts of joyful service springing from *love*.

Today's Challenge

So for today's challenge, I am giving you two options. But feel free to choose both!

Option 1. As you go about your day today and find yourself doing something for your husband, compare your feelings to those first days of love. If today were truly your first day of marriage or your first day in love with him, how would your heart feel as you fold his socks, pick up his dry cleaning, bring him a glass of water, or plug his phone into the charger? Simply consider how you felt in the beginning and compare it to how you feel today. Then try to complete your normal tasks while remembering how much you really love your husband. It might not change your husband or your schedule, but it will change how you think about serving him. It just might change your perspective. And sometimes shifting our perspective changes everything else. Below, write down some of the things you expect you will be doing for your husband today and how you might think differently about them.

Option 2. Think of one thing you could do for your husband today that you don't always have the opportunity to do. When I took this challenge for myself, I set out a clean towel in the bathroom and lit a candle for Jared before he came home from work. He works out in the oil field as a welder, and the first thing he does when he comes home is take a shower. He knows where the towels are. He knows where we keep our matches. But he doesn't usually light a candle for himself. Taking those thirty extra seconds to set out the towel and light the candle for him communicated that I wanted to do something for him—even if it was simple—without being asked or feeling obligated. Can you think of something special you can do for your husband? Write it below.

I choose option _____. I plan to serve my husband in this way today . . .

_____

_____

_____

_____

_____

_____

_____

_____

_____

TALKING TO THE FATHER

Lord, I don't want to resent the things I do for my husband. I want to serve him joyfully. I want to feel as I did in the beginning, when I enjoyed every small thing I did for him. God, help me change my heart. Please help me shift my perspective so I see the opportunities to serve him as a blessing rather than an obligation. Lord, Your Word says that You bless our obedience. And I know You have called me to be a helper for my husband just as You created Eve to be a helpmate for Adam. God, as I focus on the blessing of being the only one who gets to show my husband that he is loved in this way, I know You will bless my heart and help me find joy in this. Thank You for helping me through this process. Thank You for the changes that are already taking place in my marriage. It is in Jesus's name that I pray. Amen.

REFLECT

Which option did you choose? What was going through your mind as you were doing the challenge?

Here's what I did, and here's what I thought . . .

_____

_____

_____

_____

_____

_____

_____

When you stopped to consider your feelings as you performed daily tasks for your husband, could you see a difference between how your heart felt in the beginning and how you feel today?

I now realize . . .

_____

_____

_____

_____

_____

_____

_____

_____

_____

_____

_____

How did considering this change in your emotions affect the way you want to serve your husband from now on?

In the future . . .

_____

_____

_____

_____

_____

Reach Out Intentionally

My goal is that they may be encouraged in
heart and united in love.

— Colossians 2:2, NIV

After the last hugs were given and my kids were tucked into bed, I made my way toward the kitchen. I loaded the dishwasher and wiped down the counters. I made my final rounds of locking doors and turning off unnecessary lights. I picked up a few toys that could be tripped over in the night and moved abandoned shoes into the appropriate bedrooms. I grabbed myself a glass of water, and I walked toward my bedroom.

The scene I found when I came into the room wasn't unusual. The TV was on, and my husband was sound asleep. I carefully slipped the remote out of his hand and turned off the TV.

I felt as if I hadn't seen Jared in days. We had tag-teamed our way through dinner and bath times. He gave the baby a bottle while I spent a few minutes alone with Kolton and Kadence. He had moved our dishes to the sink and rinsed them and then made his way to our room to relax for the first time since arriving home. While we had been together all evening, I felt as if I hadn't seen him. So often our duties as mommy and daddy have us in the same house but feeling as though we cannot connect.

I don't know what evenings are like at your house, but this is our normal routine: cooking, eating, and cleaning up dinner; checking homework; packing lunches for the next day; and making sure all the kids' projects or papers are signed and ready to return to school. Consequently, there isn't much time to invest in our relationship. And I bet the same is true for you and your husband.

Your evenings might be different from mine. Maybe you or your husband has a work schedule that requires being gone in the evenings. But I would guess that no matter when your together time occurs, you don't feel as if you have had a chance to connect as you did in the beginning.

And I would bet you miss your husband. I bet you miss who you were as a couple. Don't get me wrong. Many wonderful changes happen as we grow in love with our spouses, but it is easy to lose the one-on-one attention that was abundant in the beginning. The uninterrupted conversations. The undivided attention. Quiet nights together watching television. Or even just deciding to go on a quick date because you could. I bet you miss . . . *you,* when *you* meant just the two of you.

When we first fell in love, our moments together might not have been much more exciting, but they were definitely much less exhausting. Isn't this the constant challenge of married life after children? We are with each other, but rarely do we have dedicated time to give to each other. Rarely are we ever alone together. And when we are alone, just the two of us, we are often too tired to want to really connect.

I firmly believe this creates an unhealthy cycle. When we or our husbands are too tired to connect, we begin to withdraw. The person who keeps reaching out gets tired of unreciprocated feelings, and the person who just wants to rest at the end of the day can't see why the other doesn't understand that. As one or both parties begin to withhold their love a little more, the space that creeps in between the two grows wider and wider until finally there is a fear that connecting as they did in the beginning, or even before kids, will never happen again. Have you ever felt as if you and your husband were just roommates sharing a common space and responsibilities but almost entirely disconnected emotionally from each other?

How do we keep our love alive then? How do we remind our husbands they still have our hearts when we have given so much of

our love (and time and energy!) to our children? How do we connect when there isn't any time? The reality is, getting away and
asking someone else to watch our children isn't always an option. So
what do we do? How do we show that we love each other when the
only time we have together is when we have children with us or we
are completely exhausted? While there are some aspects of married
life that cannot ever be the same once children are introduced into
the relationship, that doesn't mean our hearts have to drift apart. It
just means we need to be creative in considering all the ways we
intentionally connected when we first fell in love.

Early in our relationship Jared and I frequently sent text messages. I would send him a message saying something like "Hope
you're having a good day." Or "Just wanted to let you know that I've
been thinking about you." Or even "Miss you today." And I remember being sincerely excited when he would text back, "Miss you too.
Looking forward to seeing you tonight." Sometimes I miss feeling
that way. Don't you? I miss being excited to see his name pop up on
my phone. The messages I send my husband now are more likely to
be "Grab diapers on your way home" or "These kids are driving me
crazy."

The messages, e-mails, and texts you send now are probably
most often designed to accomplish something rather than just letting him know you're thinking about him. And *that*, that's what we
are going to try to remember.

TODAY'S CHALLENGE

When we first fell in love, we were able to connect with each other just about anytime we were together. Once we have children, we understand this scenario doesn't always work the same way. The challenge today is another easy one. Before you see your husband the next time, look for a way to let him know you are thinking about him—even if he cannot respond. If your husband has access to his cell phone while he is at work or at home taking care of the kids, send a message. If you both have a chance to check your social media accounts in the middle of the day, have a post waiting for him.

When I was completing this challenge in my own relationship, I saw my husband's truck parked at city hall, where he was in a meeting as our town's mayor. I pulled over, grabbed a pen, and wrote a note. I tucked it under his windshield wiper and left before he saw me. I had done something similar when we were dating, and repeating that action reminded my heart how much I enjoyed telling him—in the middle of the day, for no particular reason—that I love him.

If today was like the first day you fell in love, you probably wouldn't wait until you saw him next before you talked to him. You would likely reach out in some way without even thinking twice about it. A call, a text, a chat, a note.

Today remember that love. Remember how excited you were to say, "Just thinking about you," and you hoped he was feeling the same way. So let's be real for a second. Your husband might not respond the way you want him to after you complete this challenge. He might ignore the message. He might miss the gesture. He might not reply to the text. He might not "like" or acknowledge the social media post. But you are sowing seeds of love in your relationship, and I want you to remember that this process isn't about changing your husband. Right? It is about changing *how you love* your husband. We can't change our history, and we can't change our circumstances. And the reality is we cannot change our spouses. But we can change our own attitudes, and that is a very good start.

Here's how I plan to connect with my husband today . . .

_____

_____

_____

_____

_____

TALKING TO THE FATHER

Lord, I am nearly halfway through this series of challenges, and I am recognizing how much has changed in my marriage. Help me not to become discouraged as I work toward changing my perspective. Help me continue to look for ways to connect intentionally with my husband throughout the day. And as I do so, as I find opportunities to say hello or let him know that I'm thinking about him, help me realize that You desire that same type of connection with me. You want me to call on You just because I'm thinking of You. You want me to stop in my day and tell You I love You. You are forever reaching out to me. You are forever reminding me of Your unending love. Lord, help this type of love to spill over into every other relationship in my life, especially my marriage. You are good, God, and I thank You for first loving me. In Jesus's name I pray. Amen.

REFLECT

How did your husband respond when you reached out? Did he seem excited that you had reached out to him? Was it the response you wanted? How did you feel as you completed this step?

Here's how it went . . .

_____

_____

_____

_____

_____

_____

_____

_____

_____

_____

How is it going as you continue to speak kindly, greet each other, and touch intentionally? Have you been consistent? If you haven't been able to complete those daily challenges, take a deep breath, give yourself some more grace, and start again tomorrow.

What I've noticed so far as I complete these challenges is . . .

_____

_____

_____

_____

_____

_____

_____

_____

_____

_____

Day 11

Fight Fairly

Her husband can trust her,
and she will greatly enrich his life.

— Proverbs 31:11

I remember the first fight Jared and I had. It was so ridiculous that I almost don't want to share it, but I guess I will anyway. We were riding in his pickup, and I was sitting in the middle seat. Back then I couldn't stand to have even a seat between us, so we would sit side by side no matter where we went. Isn't that sweet? (Now I would settle for just sitting next to him on the couch for five minutes.) On the day of our first fight, we were in his truck getting ready to run to the store. As Jared buckled his seat belt, he accidentally pinched me. It was an honest accident, but I turned and shouted, "Ouch! You pinched me!"

He just laughed and stared blankly back at me. Laughing, I

said, "Say you're sorry! I think that's going to leave a mark!" And he replied, "I didn't mean to pinch you! It wasn't like I did it on purpose! It's not like I wanted to hurt you." We both kept laughing, but for some reason he wouldn't say he was sorry. It wasn't a big deal, but it turned into a bigger deal the longer it went on. (Fights tend to do that, don't they?)

He had apologized for silly things in the past, so it was not as if I had never heard him apologize before. But on this night, every time I asked him to say he was sorry, he would say, "You know I'm sorry. Why do I have to say it?" Now, because you weren't there with us, I need to make it clear that he was just teasing me. We both knew he was playing around, and we were both genuinely laughing about how silly it was that he wouldn't say he was sorry. But the longer it went on, the more it escalated. I wasn't upset that he pinched me. I wasn't even upset that he wouldn't say the words. I was mostly upset that he wouldn't do something just because I asked him to. (This was a preview of the next ten years of our married life. I just didn't realize it then.)

But to show how distressed I was, I unbuckled and moved to the far side of the truck. He teased back, "You're overreacting," and I replied, "You're being stubborn."

We were officially mad at each other for thirty whole minutes before he wrote down the words "I love you" on a piece of paper and slid it toward me. He apologized, and I hugged him while pleading, "Let's never fight again!"

Except that didn't happen. Our fights didn't stop. They just grew along with our relationship.

Parenthood is like the perfect storm, holding all the necessary elements to create intense arguments between a husband and wife. Jared and I discovered this shortly after we brought our first baby home from the hospital.

Like most new parents we had no idea what we were doing. We were terrified that we might do something wrong and ruin our kid forever. We were stressed as we figured out our new roles as mom and dad. And we were completely exhausted emotionally and physically from the lack of sleep and all the other changes.

On top of all that, we were doing our best to figure out everything in real time. It's not like you get a practice week with your newborn. You don't get to try out parenthood for a few days and then pass your baby back to the hospital, saying, "That felt like a good run, but let's shoot again for next week. We have some stuff we need to work out before we bring this model home."

No. The entrance into parenthood goes something like this: "Here's your new baby. No manual. Good luck."

With hope, a prayer, and a copy of the after-hours number for the pediatrician hanging on our refrigerator, we did our best to navigate our new life. But often we didn't agree. Jared wanted to do things one way, and I wanted to do things another. He was at work all day, and I was at home taking care of our baby. The stress, the changes, and the exhaustion all created plenty of moments when we just argued with each other.

Maybe the same is true at your house. Perhaps you do your very best to love your husband well, but there are still days when you disagree unkindly and have to ask for forgiveness. Parenthood is often hard on marriages, and sometimes couples fight. So how do we fight fairly?

How do we fight today as we fought in the beginning of our marriages?

1. Never use the secret places of your husband's heart against him. In the beginning of your relationship, you didn't know all your husband's deepest truths. You didn't know all his secret fears or worries or shame. But as relationships mature, we learn things about our husbands that no one else knows—areas of their hearts that they have entrusted to us alone. When we choose not to fight fairly, we may be tempted to use these secrets as daggers in dangerously futile fights.

    What do I mean? Well, think about it. The things that really bother our husbands—the fear that they won't be successful or the fear that they're not good dads or the dread that they are in dead-end jobs—are places within them that we should never, ever attack. But if we are being honest with ourselves, it can be very tempting to address these heart issues when we are upset.

In the middle of an argument, we might say just the right thing to win. But, friend, I'm sure years of marriage have already taught you that in fights like these when we use words as weapons, no one wins.

2. Don't do any name-calling. In the beginning you might have jokingly called each other a silly version of what you really wanted to say. You might have said, "Stop being such a jerk." But don't let time erode your filter, friend. Name-calling didn't win his heart, and it shouldn't be a part of your conversation today. Just make the decision right now to stop. And remember, name-calling doesn't mean just swear words. It can be as simple as a hurtful label: lazy, dumb, incompetent. Scripture reminds us in Ephesians 4:29, "Do not let any unwholesome talk come out of your mouths" (NIV). There aren't qualifications on this text either. It doesn't say, "Do not let any unwholesome talk come out of your mouth unless your husband is being a real jerk." I'm certain God's message to us here has been presented clearly and without exception.

3. Work toward a common goal. In the beginning there was no doubt you were a team working together to resolve an issue. Today a more appropriate comparison

of your disagreements might be disputes between Vikings from opposing kingdoms who take no prisoners. Friend, Scripture reminds us in Mark 10:8 that we are one flesh with our husbands. And when we tear them apart, we are really attacking ourselves. There are no sides, imaginary lines, or final death rounds. In order to prove your point, you don't have to defeat your spouse. Winning looks like reaching a mutual agreement—not trampling your opponent. You must always remember that you are working toward the same goal: creating a healthy and happy home for your family.

4. Above all, remember the permanence of your words. You may be able to clarify your words, add to them, and explain them, but you will never be able to unsay them. The words you say to your spouse today will become the foundation you stand on when communicating tomorrow. Choose each word wisely.

TODAY'S CHALLENGE

For today's challenge respond to every potential disagreement with the same love and grace you showed your spouse in the beginning. This is certainly how we acted when we first fell in love. So today when the opportunity to disagree presents itself, consider only the situation directly in front of you. Do not bring up past hurts, call names, or try to tear apart your husband's side of the argument. Look for ways to work together. Find your common ground.

Your spouse isn't your enemy. (I'm talking to myself here too.) We know this. Deep down we know there is a very real Enemy that wants nothing more than to steal, kill, and destroy our families. We know that he wants to turn us against each other. Scripture tells us this is true. But for some reason we still fight with our spouses rather than fighting together *with* our spouses. We turn our words as weapons toward each other when we should unite our words and aim them together in prayer.

So today let's flip the script. Today and tomorrow and for as long as these words carry life within us, let's cling to the truth that God has given each of us a covenant alliance in our husbands. God has given each of us a partner to stand with as we fight against hell for our families. And the minute we realize we've been tearing apart our home with our own hands, we are going to look at our children and remember that we're not fighting because of them. We are going to fight in prayer alongside our spouses *for* them.

What things do you find yourself fighting about most with your husband? Do you ever talk through these issues when you aren't in the middle of a fight? In addition to fighting fairly today, take a minute to journal your main trigger areas. Knowing which hot-button issues cause the most dissension between you and your husband can help you prepare an appropriate response when those topics or moments arise.

Here are my trigger areas I need to watch out for . . .

_____

_____

_____

_____

_____

_____

_____

_____

_____

TALKING TO THE FATHER

Lord, as I interact with my husband, help me view each encounter with fresh eyes and a fresh heart. Help me see my husband as I did when we first fell in love. Lord, I ask that You would show me how to disagree with my husband in a way that doesn't damage our relationship. When those moments of friction arise, continually remind my heart that my husband is not my enemy. Help me choose to work toward common ground so we can defeat our real Enemy. Let my words be gentle, and let my fight be for love. In Jesus's name I pray. Amen.

REFLECT

So how did it go? Was it all sunshine and rainbows, or did your husband tick you off before nine this morning? For reflection purposes, write out how using the techniques we talked about here changed the tone of the conversation. Going forward, what do you think it means to fight fairly with your husband?

Here's how it went, and here's what I plan to do in the future . . .

_____

_____

_____

_____

Day 12

Prepare Expectantly

I am my beloved's,
And his desire is for me.

— Song of Solomon 7:10, NASB

*I*t was 2005, the year I met Jared, and I had spent most of the summer lying out by the pool at the apartment complex where my momma worked. (Clearly, this was before I had any children.) This was a new job for my mom. She and my dad had moved into one of the apartments so she could manage the property after I graduated from high school and went off to college. It was in a town far away from all my friends, so when I went home for the summer after my freshman year of school, I didn't know anyone.

You know the rest of this story. Well, you know most of it. I took a job at a nearby mall to pass the time and met this guy I fell in love with. But what you don't know is that when I wasn't at the mall, I was shopping, lying out by the pool, and learning new makeup techniques. I would do my daily Bible devotionals at night, and I would journal a little while I was at work, but the rest of my time revolved around my appearance. I won't lie—a huge part of me wishes this weren't true. I mean, I could have been volunteering, serving local charities, or campaigning for organizations that I supported. But, no, it was all about me.

The summer I met my husband was the time in my life when I thought the most about my appearance. He saw me at my beauty-caring best, at a time when I was most invested in how I looked. Praise the Lord that he didn't fall for me based on my looks. (Well, praise the Lord that appearance was not the *only* reason he was interested in me.)

Ten years later I'm lucky if I get to shower every day, and it's a bonus if I have time to shave my legs. I promise it isn't because I don't care. I just don't often have the time to show how much I care. The simple reality is that I have a life lived in conjunction with the demanding schedules and lives of four other people. Trust me. I completely care that some days when I'm home with my kids, the baby wakes up before I do, and I don't get out of my pajamas until his nap time. The actual pajamas don't bother me because they are crazy comfortable. They are a sexy ensemble of my high school drama-team T-shirt and Christmas flannel pants, just in case you were wondering. So I basically look like I stepped out of a Victoria's Secret ad—only not really. But, seriously, the fact that most days I can't seem to squeeze out even ten minutes to invest in myself bothers me.

I know there are wonderful books about making time for ourselves. I know there are women who dedicate their lives to helping other women with this very issue, and their ministry is a beautiful gift. But no matter how much time we make, steal, or borrow for ourselves, it still won't compare to the endless amount of free time and "me time" we had before we had children.

This lack of time to invest in ourselves can put a strain on how we feel our husbands perceive us. I mean, my husband thinks I'm beautiful no matter what I'm wearing and no matter how much of yesterday's makeup is still on my face. But how I feel about how I look—and how I feel about how I think he thinks I look—affects me and affects us.

I want to look the way I did in 2005. I want to take long showers with exfoliating shower gels and color-preserving shampoos and deep conditioners. I want to shave my legs and paint my toenails and fingernails and get my eyebrows waxed. I want to put on lotion and skin-smoothing face creams and blow-dry and style my hair. But most days when I have free time to fix myself up, I'd rather do something else . . . like rest.

When my husband comes home from work, and I have a sloppy ponytail, am wearing last night's pj's, and can't remember if I brushed my teeth, I know I'm a mess. More than anything else, I just want him to see past it.

But when I think about it, I want him to know that I wish I could still be that girl who had time to care about herself as I did back then, not just because she wanted to look nice, but because she wanted to look nice *for him.* I wonder if you ever feel that way. Whether you stay at home with your kids or go to work, do you ever feel that you don't have the time to invest in your appearance as you once did? Do you ever wonder if your husband thinks about it?

I tried this experiment a few months ago as I was preparing to write this challenge. During the kids' nap time, I showered and fixed my hair. About ten minutes before my husband usually comes home from work, I put on a little makeup and a cute outfit. Just for him.

Yes, I had run errands all day in my sweats. I had taken my son to school wearing my classic mommy morning style that I think is best described as "Lord, don't let anyone see me." But when I knew my husband was just minutes away, I ran and dressed as if preparing myself to see him was the most important event in my day. I even put on heels.

And do you know what happened? Well, Jared was late getting home from work, and I had to stay in those stinkin' shoes until seven thirty because I never knew when he was going to walk through the door. But when he finally did walk in, and I greeted him as I had been practicing, he said, "You look really nice."

That was it. It wasn't this big, elaborate "Wow! My love! What have you done?! What is this lipstick you are wearing?! Surely this is the bride of my youth!" I would be lying if I said I wasn't hoping he would make a big deal about it. But he noticed. And the fact that he said anything made me realize he pays attention.

I know that not every momma is where I am when it comes to having limited time to care for herself. You might be reading these words with a turned-up nose as you think that you would never go days without showering. But stick with me for a second, because this challenge is for all of us.

TODAY'S CHALLENGE

In creating today's challenge I thought, *What would my dad do?* If this entire challenge is based on the idea that my dad treats each day as if he were a newlywed, then how does my dad prepare to see my mom? Well, every morning he gets dressed and ready to impress her, and that means he shaves his face daily. Why? It's simple. My mom likes a clean-shaven face. Whether it is the middle of the week or the weekend, he doesn't take a day off. He shaves his face just because he loves her.

No, this challenge isn't about facial hair. I'm asking you to think about what you did to prepare to see your husband when you first fell in love with him. I'm talking about the very beginning. What were some of the things you did? I imagine that whether your efforts were elaborate or simple, they were intentional in whatever way was comfortable to you. I'm not saying you have to put on makeup if you don't usually. I'm not saying you need to wear clothing that isn't practical. Heaven knows, babies and earrings and soccer practice and heels don't always mix.

Practically, I know you may not have the time to invest the way you did in the beginning. I sure don't. But for today's challenge I would love for you to prepare to greet your husband tonight as you would have if he were taking you on a date. As I said, it doesn't have to be elaborate. This challenge is simply about being intentional. We know that our husbands love us no matter how we look. One of the joys of marriage is that with our spouses we can be comfortable with who we really are. But just for fun today (or for as long as you feel like doing this), get ready to see your husband as if it were the first day you fell in love.

Here's what I'm going to do . . .

_____

_____

_____

_____

_____

TALKING TO THE FATHER

Lord, as I'm spending these days refocusing my attention on my marriage, remembering what it was like in the beginning, I thank You for the simple effort I can make every day that reflects the bigger intentions of my heart. Setting aside time to take care of myself is one of these changes. God, I know I'm worth my own attention. Help me find ways to set time aside to care for myself. And, Lord, even though I know my husband loves me no matter how I look, help me rediscover joy in delighting him. I want to remember how fun it was to prepare myself to see him. In Jesus's name I pray. Amen.

REFLECT

Well, what did you do? Did you shave your legs? Did you throw on a dress? Maybe you just brushed your teeth and combed your hair. My question for you is this: No matter what you chose to do, did you notice a change in how *you* felt? Did the effort to be intentional change how you felt about seeing your husband? Did he notice? What was his response? Take a minute to journal your thoughts for this challenge.

Here's what happened . . .

_____

_____

_____

_____

_____

_____

_____

_____

What are some of the things you are praying for your marriage? What are some of the issues or needs you are bringing before the Lord right now?

_____

_____

_____

_____

_____

_____

_____

_____

_____

_____

_____

_____

Day 13

Honor Consistently

Be devoted to one another in love. Honor
one another above yourselves.

— Romans 12:10, NIV

I went to school at Oral Roberts University in Tulsa, Oklahoma. If you don't know much about the university, let me quickly fill you in on a few things. ORU is a small, private Christian university that enforces many rules concerning dress code, moral behavior, and chapel and class attendance. They impose a strict curfew, and in order to stay off campus for the weekend, you must first sign out. At least, this was true ten years ago. The overall campus isn't what I would describe as huge. All these factors and the shared views and common faith of many of the students and faculty create a tight-knit community.

So when I returned from summer vacation with stories about a boy I had met "off campus," which meant he wasn't a part of our ORU family, everyone wanted to hear all about him. "What is he like?" "Where did you meet?" "Does he love Jesus?" "Is he going to come to ORU too?" "When are you getting married?" It's a running joke on campus that if you fall in love before Christmas, you will have a ring by spring. So, naturally, my friends were already discussing bridesmaid dresses.

Since Jared was not planning to attend ORU and lived more than a hundred miles away, the only way my friends knew anything about him was through my stories. So I did my very best to tell everyone just how wonderful Jared was. I told them about all the kind things he had done for me. I told them all about the greatest adventures, like the time we went to a minor league baseball game and the kiss cam focused on us. I was bashful since the entire stadium was watching, and he was kind and patient, but after a few seconds I leaned in, and the entire crowd cheered. For as long as I live, I hope I never forget that when I looked up, I saw that not only were the people in the stands cheering but one of the outfielders had tucked his glove under his arm and was clapping too. It was like something out of a movie.

I told them how Jared started coming to church with my family. I shared stories about how we spent day after day together because he was so fun and made me laugh. And I made sure to share only the very best parts of him. Not because I was purposefully omitting the not-so-great parts, but because I cared about how my friends viewed him. Jared was a wonderful guy whom I cared for, and I wanted them to think highly of him too.

I bet you were probably the same way when it came to introducing your future husband to your friends and family. You minimized his not-so-great points while focusing on all his strengths. You can probably anticipate my next question: Do you still speak as highly of your husband today? To everyone?

A few years ago Jared and I were in the middle of a pretty ugly fight. I don't remember what it was about, probably something important like whose job it was to feed the dog. But I was so upset that I called my friend. "You won't believe what Jared is doing! He is driving me crazy! Listen to this . . ." I proceeded to tell her all the terrible things Jared had done and then expected her to affirm that I was right and he was wrong and was just a terrible guy. And while I was on the phone, I will admit that I felt better. "See! He's so awful. He's just the worst. I just don't know how I can keep going with him acting like this. I just don't know what I'm going to do to get over this."

But eventually Jared and I made up. We got past it. I don't remember how we made up, but it was apparently resolved to the point that I don't even remember what we were fighting about back then. The problem was, I had to call my friend and try to take back all the things I had said. I had to try to unsay them, and we all know how well that works. I had to tell her how Jared was sorry and how he wasn't going to do, or say, or act that way anymore. I had to convince her that he was a good guy. I had to try to redeem his name, the same name I had torn apart with my own words.

Not only have I watched as my dad has worked to protect my mom's name and reputation, but I have also witnessed him purposely honor her publically. Whenever he is introducing her, he presents her as "my beautiful wife, Susan." Never once have I heard him speak badly of her or say how wrong she is. Which is annoying at times, because when I go to my dad to complain about a disagreement I have with my mom, he always sides with her. *Always.* Not most of the time. Not when he is in a good mood. Not just when he sees the validity of her argument. Always. Because she is his wife, he fights to uphold her reputation, refusing to be one to hurt her.

Look, I know that in the moment it feels good to be validated in what we are experiencing with our spouses, but we can never unsay the things we share with others outside our marriages. We should do our very best to protect the reputation of our spouses at all times, because rarely do we have the opportunity or ability to fully mend what we have broken.

This includes what we say to our children. We teach our children how to interact with the world through what they experience at home. How will our children learn to honor their father if they don't see their momma modeling that for them? If we want them to grow up understanding the importance of respect, we have to do our very best to teach them how to honor those in authority—and this includes their dad.

How would you speak about your husband to others if it were the first day you fell in love with him? You probably would not say, "He's an idiot. He always forgets our anniversary. And he never does anything to help around the house." Instead, you might say, "He does so many things well. He's a good guy. He's a kind man. He's a great _____." It isn't about being untruthful. It is about remembering the power that our words have to shape the opinions of others. And sometimes saying the words out loud changes our opinion as well.

Today's Challenge

If you were going to speak about your husband today the way you did when you first fell in love, what would you say? And, sister, what wouldn't you say? Today—all day—and then for the rest of this challenge, we are going to be intentional about what we share and do not share about our husbands. Today create one moment, whether with your children, your friends, or your extended family, to compliment and honor your husband. We are going to do our best not to share our husbands' faults with others, and we are going to actively praise and honor them instead.

Please note that if you are in a situation that needs professional counsel, do not hesitate to share the full truth about your situation with your counselor. This challenge should never be used in place of the advice of a licensed professional counselor. If you are facing an abusive situation, please tell someone.

Positive things I will share about my husband are . . .

_____

_____

_____

_____

_____

_____

_____

_____

Talking to the Father

Lord, I know You ask me to honor my husband. I know that honor is important to You and an important part of the culture of the kingdom of heaven. Help me choose to show respect to my husband continually, no matter the state of my heart. Help me build him up always, not just to his face, but in conversations with others as well. Above all, remind me of the importance of guarding my husband's character. I know we all fall short of perfection. Because we live in a broken world, we don't always make the best choices, but help me see my husband's less-than-perfect moments as opportunities to extend grace. Help me see him as You see him and share that view of him with everyone I know. In Jesus's name I pray. Amen.

REFLECT

How did it go? Were you able to complete the challenge today? Did you refrain from calling your mom or his mom or your best friend the second he did something to make you angry? Did you show honor and respect to your husband in front of your children? What happened as a result? Why do you feel as though this is or is not something that could impact your marriage?

Here's how it went . . .

_____

_____

_____

Day 14

Correct Sparingly

For we live by faith, not by sight.

—2 Corinthians 5:7, NIV

When Kolton was born, Jared changed his diapers in the hospital. I was breast-feeding, so Jared thought that changing Kolton's diapers was one way he could contribute to caring for our newborn. (And I wasn't going to fight him for that job.) It was wonderful. Parenting together was a breeze. But somewhere between shoving our "Congratulations on Your Baby Boy" balloons into the car with us and Kolton's first bath, chaos broke loose. I didn't know how many ways my husband could be "wrong" until we had babies.

For example, I had never seen a man who could bathe a newborn so incorrectly. Of course, Jared argued that he had been the one to watch the nurse bathe Kolton while I slept in the hospital, so clearly he knew how to give our newborn a bath. Except I had read that babies' skin is so sensitive that even mildly warm water can scald them (or something ridiculous like that). Jared was telling me it was fine to hold Kolton over the kitchen sink and pour water over him, and I was desperately trying to make Jared lay our very breakable baby down on the padded foam bath sponge I had bought so we could bathe him as I had planned.

Similar fights occurred over the next six years. Because, as I said, when it came to taking care of our babies, that man did more things wrong than I had thought humanly possible. I found myself constantly correcting him. I wanted to always be right.

"Those aren't the right pajamas. They are too tight on his toes."

"We are in size three diapers now; they are in the bottom drawer. I kept the old ones in case I ran out of the bigger ones . . . No, I don't want to use those up, because they leak since they are too small. No, I don't want to throw them away because they are better than nothing in case I run out completely!"

"She doesn't like that paci. I don't know why. She just fusses, but she doesn't seem to fuss with this one. Here. Give her this one. See. Yep, now she's upset!"

Couldn't he get anything right?!

Not surprisingly he felt the exact same way about me. Our parenting became stressful. The atmosphere in the house was tense. We waged a continual tug of war over how things *should* be done.

Until eventually my husband sort of backed away. He didn't

fight me as hard, but he also seemed a little disengaged. I felt stuck in this terrible place of wanting my husband to be involved while also feeling as though it would be easier if he went back to work so I could do it my way without his being, well, in my way. It wasn't good. Those aren't nice thoughts. That's not a healthy environment or relationship.

So I would try to let him do it his way. I would try not to step in and *just do it* simply because it was easier and it was what the kids were used to. I *tried*.

But ultimately, I always seemed to end up taking care of it myself.

This wasn't much like things were in the beginning of our relationship. We did everything together when we first fell in love. I loved to hear his opinion on things. I valued what he thought. I sought out better ways to do what I was doing, and I believed that Jared would have trustworthy insight. But we didn't have kids back then either.

Sure, I didn't always agree with him, and there were certainly plenty of moments when I wanted to correct him. But back then I didn't correct him every chance I could. I didn't tell him how wrong I thought he was. Because letting him know that his opinion mattered to me was more important than being right.

So how do we go back in this case? How do we look at this situation and treat our husbands as if it were the first day we fell in love with them? How do we keep ourselves from trying to correct them constantly? Or even thinking of how we might want to correct them?

We have to begin by acknowledging a few things. There are at least two people parenting your child. You and your husband. And as much as you now wish he thought, acted, or felt like you, he is a unique person. He isn't like you in many ways, and that is okay. Just because he doesn't do something the way you would doesn't make it wrong. So what if he puts on the wrong size diaper? So what if he gives the baby another jar of fruit instead of a veggie? What harm will result if bath time comes and goes and he hasn't used a washcloth once? If he doesn't give your child the advice you would give? If he doesn't help with the school project the way you would?

Constantly correcting our husbands is just as destructive as continually nagging them, because it conveys our lack of faith in our husbands' decisions. But when we extend grace in the form of trust, we communicate to our husbands that we don't have to be in complete control. We can trust them with our children, and we can trust them to make other wise choices as well.

Today's Challenge

Today we will treat our husbands as if it were the first day we fell in love with them by correcting them sparingly. We will ask ourselves a few questions before we try to change our husbands' actions, words, or beliefs. Is what they are doing dangerous? If we don't correct them, will they still reach the same outcome or a similar outcome as they would if we corrected them? Will our words bring more harm than good? As we consider the answers to these questions, we continue to build and exercise trust that will lead us into a deeper level of love. I am forever taking deep breaths and reminding myself that I don't have to be right . . . even if I *know* I'm right.

The things my husband does that I would do differently are . . .

_____

_____

_____

_____

_____

_____

_____

_____

Talking to the Father

Lord, thank You for trusting me to make good choices. I know I don't always make the best ones, but I try. Just as You extend grace toward me, giving me the freedom to figure things out, help me extend that same love toward my husband. Help me remember that You direct him and guide him just as You direct me and guide me. You won't let either of us down. So I will trust You to lead my husband and to help me remember to put my faith where it belongs—in a man who can make good choices and a God who has yet to fail me. God, help me correct my heart when I'm focused more on being right than on building my relationship. In Jesus's name I pray. Amen.

Reflect

Did you keep track of how many things your husband did today that you would have done differently? How did you respond to these differences of opinion? Were you able to use the questions to gauge your response?

Here's how it went . . .

_____

_____

_____

_____

_____

_____

Do you believe that giving your husband the freedom to make his own choices without your input will communicate love to him? How do you think this challenge will impact your marriage going forward?

_____

_____

_____

_____

_____

_____

_____

Day 15

Choose Wisely

This time I don't want to make just a short
visit and then go right on. I want to come
and stay awhile, if the Lord will let me.

— 1 Corinthians 16:7

*I*t was a simple text message: "Do you want to go on a run
with me?" And without even thinking twice about my answer, I replied, "Absolutely. When?"

When Jared and I met, I might have tried to be a little more
interesting than I really was. Remember, I spent my free time reading devotionals and thinking about clothing. I didn't have any hobbies I was particularly consumed with (unless getting a suntan
counts). I didn't have any real talent I could boast of. And I didn't
even have any friends nearby. So when Jared asked what I did with

all my free time, I tried to sound interesting by offering my list of what I hoped to learn or experience by the end of the summer.

When the summer began, I had made a sheet of goals I wanted to complete before returning to school in August. On the list were things like learn to play the guitar, pick up golf, and develop a work-out routine. I just had to get past my procrastination first. So I started with running (I mean jogging), because people who run seem to have their lives together. Have you ever noticed this? Are you a runner? I don't think I've ever met a lazy marathon runner. But surely every marathon runner began with jogging.

So when Jared asked me what I liked to do, I included running, even though I had made it around the apartment complex only twice by that point. I explained, "Yeah, I like to run, but I don't do it often, because I think it can be dangerous to run alone in a college town like this." Jared used this opportunity and said, "Well, maybe we could run together sometime." And with that, we had planned our first unofficial date.

It wasn't until his text message came that I wondered what I had gotten myself into. I don't actually run! I die! I run out of breath, out of energy, out of motivation. And then I run to get a pizza. But this didn't cause me to say no when he asked me to come over, because my decision wasn't based on what Jared had asked me to do. I said yes because I wanted to spend time with him. It wasn't about what we did together. It was about being together.

Just so you know the rest of the story, I'll confess that we barely made it to the end of his street before I felt as if I was going to pass out. He literally took my hand and led me back to his house while I gasped for breath and told him I hated running. To this day his parents tease me about how much I like to jog.

I might not have been into running, but if this told Jared anything, it was that I wanted to be around him. He could be confident that our time together was valuable to me. He could be sure that I would readily choose to spend time with him. And for the rest of the summer, that is exactly what we did. We chose each other. We were inseparable.

But the truth is, I'm not as quick to choose Jared today. I miss spending time with him. But I wish that I missed him enough to pick him over time alone or time catching up on what I need to get done. While I miss our time alone together, I'm guilty of choosing other things before Jared. He doesn't ask me on as many dates as he used to when we first fell in love, although we have regular date nights as often as our schedules and our baby-sitters will allow. There aren't the fun text messages that say, "Let's go running!" He doesn't ask if I want to spend time with him. But he probably shouldn't have to.

Now that we are well into our marriage, Jared doesn't say, "Let's get together tonight and watch TV. I'll make the popcorn." He might shout from our bedroom, "*Late Night* is on. Do you want to watch it with me?" But even this is rare, because after you get married, there is a standing invitation to spend time with each other.

You have promised for your entire lives, from now until death, to be together. I think sometimes we take that time for granted. *I have all eternity to spend with this dude, and tonight I need to get these dishes done . . . or to catch up on the laundry.*

When I think about it, when I take today and fold it over on the timeline of our marriage and compare it to the beginning, I can see how differently we feel about spending time with each other. Yes, we enjoy being together. Yes, we wish we could go on dates more often. Yes, I still like him. But right now I choose things over him more than at any other time in our relationship.

Let's be honest. Suppose our future husbands had called us on the phone when we first started dating and said, "Do you want to spend time together tonight? I don't have to work." Would we have replied, "Nah. I'm good. I'm just going to sit here on my couch and scroll through Facebook for hours"? Or, "No, I really need to get caught up on *The Bachelor* or play on Pinterest"? I'm not saying we never declined an invitation to spend time together. I'm saying we generally didn't say no just so we could do things that were far less important.

But that is exactly what we do now. Because while he might not be asking, the invitation is always there.

I think the best example of this standing invitation is my parents' evening routine. They often spend quiet time together in the same room doing different things, but when one of them is tired and is ready to go to bed, the other one goes as well. It's not a declared invitation. One of them doesn't say, "Will you come with me now?" It's just a simple routine they have established. They choose each other, every single time, over another TV show, newspaper article, or laundry pile.

So what would this look like in our relationships? How could we make choosing our husbands as effortless? And why would we want to? Let's try this.

What if today you took every opportunity to choose your husband over everything else? I know it is almost impossible to tell our children to wait. Babies aren't patient waiters, toddlers aren't patient waiters, even our teenagers aren't always patient when it comes to waiting. I know that our schedules sometimes require us to choose other things over time with our husbands, and we don't have a say in the matter. I'm not telling you to neglect your baby or miss a ball game that's important to your high school son or daughter. I am saying we need to become better about identifying the moments when we do have the choice and then choosing wisely.

Are the kids in bed? Do you just want to sit and stare mindlessly without anyone touching you? Take a deep breath, find your husband, and just be near him. It doesn't have to involve talking, touching, planning, or anything else. It is just intentional time. Today let's imagine that he has already asked the question, "Do you want to spend time with me?" And then let's find a way to say yes.

Yes, he will still be there tomorrow, but what if we viewed that as a promise rather than an excuse? He will be there tomorrow, the next day, and the next, and if we want to continue to see fruit from the investment we make in our relationship, we need to keep planting seeds. But that requires clearing space and preparing the soil of our hearts.

Today's Challenge

Today's challenge is fairly straightforward. We are going to choose time with our husbands every chance we get.

What are some practical realities that make choosing your husband seem impossible? What about the moments when you just don't want to spend time with him? What are some of the things you prefer to do alone? Do you think it will be hard to choose him over those things?

Take a minute to explain why, in your situation, choosing him isn't always possible.

_____

_____

_____

_____

_____

_____

_____

_____

_____

_____

Now take a minute to brainstorm a way in the middle of that madness to say one yes.

Here is how I am going to put my husband first today . . .

_____

_____

_____

_____

_____

_____

_____

_____

_____

_____

_____

_____

TALKING TO THE FATHER

Lord, my day is full of choices. You understand this already. You know how many options and decisions I am faced with continually. Sometimes I'm overwhelmed by all the choices I must make. But, God, I thought when I decided to marry my husband, he was one choice I would never have to make again. I thought I would say yes to marrying him and would never have to think about saying yes to that question again. But the truth is, Lord, I make the choice daily to commit fully to our marriage. Choosing my husband is something I do over and over again. God, I ask that You would help me see the moments that make up my yes. Help me recognize each opportunity to spend time with my husband, and help me remember that each of these decisions to spend time together creates my much stronger yes. In the name of Jesus, I pray. Amen.

Reflect

How did it go? Did you find opportunities to choose your husband? Did you find yourself looking for opportunities to spend time with him? What happened?

Here's what happened today . . .

_____

_____

_____

_____

_____

_____

_____

_____

_____

_____

By now you're likely familiar with these prompts, but I want to ask you something new. How is everything else in your life right now? We are journaling through these twenty-one days, and I believe the answers we spill out here will be a tremendous encouragement in the future as we look back and see all that God has done. But as you share your heart about your marriage, take a second to do a quick three-sixty around your life, looking at the other aspects that surround your relationship. These factors often affect other areas of our lives, including our marriages. What else is going on right now? How are you doing?

_____

_____

_____

_____

_____

_____

_____

_____

Day 16

Connect Intimately

How much better is your love than wine.

—Song of Solomon 4:10, NASB

I sat nervously in the doctor's office waiting for the nurse to call my name. I had been there seemingly hundreds of times over the last three years. First with Kolton and then when I was pregnant with Kadence. But when Kadence was six months old, I decided to go back and see my ob-gyn again. Not because I was pregnant, but because I was worried that something might be wrong. I just wasn't interested in being intimate—at all—and it was taking a toll on my marriage.

As I sat there, I wondered how the kids were doing back at my mom's house. She had agreed to watch them for the afternoon. It was nice having a break since I was with them all the time. With a two-year-old and a six-month-old, rarely did I get time alone. The trip to the doctor's office was like a minivacation.

They called my name, and I followed the nurse back to the exam room. It was so different this visit. I wasn't waddling down the halls or leaving samples in the bathroom. I was just waiting to visit with the doctor to figure out what my problem might be. And, hopefully, to find a solution. Perhaps there were hormonal supplements I could take. Perhaps she would recommend counseling or something. Since Kadence had come along, things had been so rough between Jared and me. It wasn't just the stress of the new baby; it was balancing it all—adjusting to life with two under two, establishing my routine again, and trying to remember how to be a wife in the middle of all of it. On top of everything else, I felt as if my body were broken. I wanted to be interested in sex, but no matter how hard I tried, I just wasn't. Whatever the solution was, I prayed that my doctor would help me find it.

We spent the first few minutes talking about my children. We discussed how old they were and joked about whether we were considering baby number three. She asked how Kolton was adjusting to having a little sister at home and how I was adjusting to being a mom of two. Once we were all caught up, she sat down on her rolling chair and pulled it closer to me. "So what's really going on?" she asked, knowing I hadn't made the appointment because I missed her.

"Well," I said, a little embarrassed, "I'm just not interested in sex anymore, and I feel so bad about it." There it was. My secret uncovered. I hadn't even talked to my husband about it. He knew I wasn't interested, but we didn't talk about it. We just ignored it. Or maybe I was the only one ignoring it. I felt ashamed that I was even in the office, but with my heart exposed, I waited for her answer. Maybe she could give me something that would help my marriage.

I remember she smiled a little, lifted her glasses off her face, and tucked them into her blond hair. She leaned in and said, "Becky, sweetheart, there's nothing wrong with you. You're just tired."

And I cried. I cried so hard that I had to cover my face and wait to catch my breath. Because she was so right. I wasn't broken. I was exhausted. I didn't need medicine. I needed a nap. And there is something about someone else looking at you and really seeing you that makes you feel as if it is okay to fall apart. There is something about being told that you're going to be okay that gives you permission to exhale.

More than anything I didn't want to let anyone down. I wanted to feel that I was enough. That my love was enough. That what I had to give was enough. But while I felt as though I was finding a rhythm with my kids, I couldn't seem to remember how to connect intimately with Jared.

The truth is, my feelings toward him had little to do with what happened in our bedroom. It was what took place all day before I reached our bedroom door that made anything on the other side of it feel impossible.

This isn't the case just with new or young mommies. Making time for and being intentional about connecting intimately with our husbands can feel like one more thing on our to-do lists at any point of motherhood. But I think the early years create so much space between husbands and wives. Not only are we exhausted, but we often have other people in bed with us—babies who are nursing or littles who are sleeping with us. Even families who enforce strict independent sleep routines might still have a child who has a bad dream and crawls in between mommy and daddy.

In addition to this, many of us have to come to terms with our postbaby bodies. We don't see the same woman we saw in the mirror on our wedding day. And as we wrestle with our own feelings concerning our new bodies, we also have to work through what we think our husbands are thinking of our new bodies. We might not be less confident overall, but there is a shift in how we feel about how we look.

On top of all of it, most days we just don't feel sexy. I wouldn't ever say being a mommy is a sexy job. As a matter of fact, on those days when I was unshowered, with unshaved legs, unfixed hair, and unbrushed teeth, the last thing I wanted was to get undressed and make love. I would much rather have put on a pair of my husband's athletic shorts and crawled into bed.

And if we can get past all these challenges, we know what

happens on the nights we say yes. We have to be quiet because the baby is sleeping in the next room or in the bassinet. And we have to be quick in case someone wakes up and needs us (and kills the mood forever). Or we wonder if our older kids are really asleep.

Look, we all know that what happens on the other side of your bedroom door matters in your marriage. We know that sex is important. We know that connecting intimately in some way with our husbands is vital. We know they have needs, and we have needs, and God created us to fulfill those needs together, but we also know that children have a way of remaking the marriage bed.

Friend, this entire book has focused on what it would look like to love today as we did on the first day we fell in love or the first days of our marriages. I think one of the clearest differences between day one and today is our intimacy with our husbands. When we first fell in love, no one had to tell us to take off the nursing bra and sweatpants and bring sexy back. No one had to tell us to find five minutes to be alone together. I don't know about you, but the day we said, "I do" . . . Well, I suppose I don't have to tell everything. Let's just say no one had to tell us, "I know you're busy. Try to have sex tonight."

The truth is, the love we showed each other in all other areas kindled the fire of our desire in the bedroom. So now that we are at this point in the process of rediscovering our marriages in the midst of motherhood, we are ready to take the intimacy challenge.

TODAY'S CHALLENGE

I want you to think about sex with your husband. Describe what sex was like when you were first married. How often did you have sex? Who initiated it? Was it spontaneous?

Sex used to be . . .

_____

_____

_____

_____

_____

_____

_____

_____

_____

_____

Describe your sex life now, answering the same questions. Who initiates sex? How frequently?

Now sex is . . .

_____

_____

_____

_____

_____

_____

_____

_____

_____

_____

Sometimes taking a minute to make a quick assessment of what has changed can be the best starting place for moving forward. Now that we can clearly see the difference, even in just the desire or energy level, here is our challenge. If you have the opportunity, and you are able and comfortable with it, make it a priority to be intimate with your husband as often as you can. It might mean you have to make finding alone time a priority. But, friend, can we be real for a second? We both know that it is the heart behind the action that makes the love.

I'm not telling you to have sex with your husband tonight (but if you're inspired to, fantastic). I'm not even telling you to be intimate with him (even though I believe some form of intimacy is so important to the health of any marriage). I am simply asking you to remember the importance of intimacy in your marriage and then do something about it.

TALKING TO THE FATHER

Lord, You created my husband and me to be one. You designed us for intimacy with each other, but often the demands of the day keep us from connecting the way I wish we could. You care about all aspects of our relationship, Lord, and that means You care about this area too. I pray that You would fan the flame of love in my heart for my husband. I pray that You would help us find opportunities to connect with each other intimately. And I ask that as we put our trust in You, You will bring our hearts together. Thank You for loving me when I don't deserve it. Thank You for continuing to pursue my heart always. Help me remember to show my husband the same kind of love over and over again. In Jesus's name I pray. Amen.

REFLECT

What has changed the most about your sex life since those early days of love? What is the reason for the change? How do you feel about it? Have you had a conversation about this with your husband? Going forward, how do you think that open communication would impact your intimate relationship with your husband?

What I want to say to my husband about our sex life is . . .

_____

_____

_____

_____

_____

_____

_____

_____

_____

_____

Earlier in this process we began touching our husbands on purpose. Did continuing that challenge contribute to your connection with him today?

_____

_____

_____

_____

_____

_____

_____

_____

Day 17

Join In Willingly

How good and pleasant it is

when God's people live together in unity!

— Psalm 133:1, NIV

efore I met Jared, I had preconceived ideas about racecar fans. My dad was not a racing fan, nor did many of my friends care much about racing. So I'm not sure how I formed my opinions. Truthfully, I didn't know a lot about it. But I did know that the fans were dedicated, and many seemed to have a favorite driver to whom they pledged their support by placing a decal on the rear window of their vehicles. Personally, I didn't get it. I didn't see the excitement in watching cars drive around for hours. I didn't think badly of racing fans, but I never saw myself as one of them. If you had told me back then that ten years later I would have watched more than a hundred Formula 1 races with my husband, I might have prayed for the Lord to pick a different guy for me.

But here we are. A decade has passed, and not only can I name most of the drivers, but I can also tell you most of their teams and sponsors. Do you know why? Because my husband is a fan of racing, and I guess that means I am too.

Do you remember when you first fell in love with your husband and wanted to know all about him? You took an interest in the things he enjoyed. I didn't do this just with Jared. I had done this with every guy I had dated before Jared. In high school you could tell the type of guy I was dating by the CD I was listening to in my car. Have you ever noticed how certain types of guys listen to certain types of music? While I had my own favorites, I would also do my best to like their preference of music as well. Some of those guys had weird tastes in music (which is probably why it didn't work out between us). But there is a reason that I tried to like what they liked. I wanted them to know they were interesting to me. I wanted to be interested in their interests.

So when Jared came on the scene, I did my very best to dive right in and find out the things he enjoyed. I already wanted to learn how to play golf, but Jared being a golfer made me much more interested. What about you? Did you take up any sudden interests when you fell for your husband? Did you find yourself watching football games and cheering for a team you knew nothing about?

Or maybe your husband loves Star Wars and you were ashamed to admit you had never seen any of the movies. Maybe it was skiing, spending time at the lake, or being outdoors in general. Whatever your husband was interested in, my guess is you tried to learn as much as you could about it.

But as time passes, we often find ourselves caring less about the things that matter to our husbands. Unfortunately, this is true for me.

Jared is supertechnical. He is the media coordinator at our church. He helps facilitate the management of the lights, sound, video, and all other recorded media. Right now I spend my time at church occasionally serving in the two- and three-year-old class. When I come upstairs from the nursery after picking up my own kids from their classes, I have stories of how we sang "Jesus Loves Me," and Jared has stories about a cue that didn't work right on some video switch or a camera that malfunctioned.

Most of the time when he talks about the technical side of his ministry at the church, it goes right over my head. I just don't get it. Don't misunderstand—I care, and I could comprehend it if I tried harder to be interested. Remember, we are working on really listening to our husbands. I'm just admitting that I don't put in the necessary effort to understand what he is trying to explain to me because it just doesn't interest me. And I know this bothers him.

It bothers me when he does the same thing to me. When I am

trying to tell him what happened at home that day or what a certain friend said, he hears me, but I can tell he doesn't really care. And then I feel that he's not interested in me. And, honestly, there is some truth to that. Because when we compare how we felt about the things that mattered to our spouses when we first fell in love with how we feel now about those things, there is a clear difference. We don't give the same level of attention that we used to give to each other's interests. Consequently, we are communicating that their interests are not worth our time.

You might do this and not even realize it. Your husband comes home from work and tells you about his day. You listen for highlights, but you don't care enough to be able to recall later how he felt about those stories he shared. Or your husband might have taken up a sudden interest in bicycling (like my husband), and you are thinking, *If I had free time, I would not climb on a tiny bike and pedal fifty miles. I would sit with a magazine and a cup of coffee and do nothing.*

When we decide we want to live as though it were the first day we fell in love, it means turning our hearts back toward our husbands' hearts. It means being interested in them—the things they enjoy, the topics they find fascinating, their friends, their work life. When we barely have five minutes to connect with our husbands throughout the day, being interested in their entire lives can feel impossible. But there has to be a place to start.

Today's Challenge

Being interested in your husband's interests now might not look the same as it did when you first fell in love. As a matter of fact, it might look very little like it did back then. So here are a few practical ways to show your husband that you are still interested in him and his interests.

1. Find a way to participate in what he spends his free time doing.

   For example, Jared often works at the church to get light settings where they need to be for the service the following week. When I can, the kids and I will run up to the church to see Daddy and take him dinner if he's going to be working late. This doesn't convey just that I want to spend time with him; it also says that what's important to him is important to me too.

2. Look for a way to connect with his friends.

   Have you considered having his friends over for a cookout some weekend? I haven't, but I know that connecting with our husbands' friends is just one more way to say what is important to them is important to us, and that includes the people in their lives.

3. Listen attentively so you can recall what your husband
   tells you about his day at work.

   While you might not ever need to know the
   different accounts your husband has been managing or
   which coworkers aren't getting along, the fact that your
   husband cares enough to share that information with
   you should make it valuable and worth remembering.

So your challenge today is open for discussion. I don't know what life is like at your house, but you do. And I'm sure that as you were reading, you were making a list in your head of some things your husband is interested in. Write that list here. What are a few things that matter to your husband that you also might be able to show interest in?

The things that matter to my husband are . . .

_____

_____

_____

_____

_____

_____

_____

_____

Now that you have made your list of your husband's interests, take time to brainstorm a way to show him that you are still invested in the things that matter to him today. Write out your thoughts below.

I'm going to show him I'm still interested by . . .

_____

_____

_____

_____

_____

_____

_____

_____

_____

_____

_____

_____

_____

Talking to the Father

Lord, thank You for the gift of my husband. As I have made this journey of rediscovering our marriage, I realize that You knew what You were doing when You brought him into my life. We are different people with sometimes different interests, but help me stay fully engaged with my husband. Help me show him I am still interested in him. That I'm still excited about the things that excite him. That I enjoy what he enjoys—because I love him. And, God, I pray that You would become a common interest between my husband and me. I pray that our love for You would be one area where we can easily connect with each other. In the name of Jesus, I pray. Amen.

Reflect

Okay, friend, how did it go? Were you able to connect with your husband in a way that allowed you to convey you were interested in him? What was your husband's response to your actions? How do you think that connecting in this way with your husband will impact your marriage?

Here's how it went . . .

_____

_____

_____

_____

_____

_____

_____

_____

_____

_____

_____

_____

_____

Day 18

Profess Passionately

Out of the abundance of the heart [the]
mouth speaks.

— Luke 6:45, esv

I was holding the phone up to my ear one second, and the next I had thrown it across the kitchen as if it had burst into flames. I didn't mean to say it! I mean, I meant the words, but I didn't realize that I meant them, and I certainly didn't mean to say them at that exact moment. *Out loud.* Those words just sort of slipped out. I couldn't control them. God was right when He said that out of the abundance of the heart the mouth speaks. Because my heart was full, and before I could put a lid on my emotions to contain them, I had professed my affections. I had told Jared, "I love you." And I don't think I was prepared for what that would mean.

It was September of 2005, and I had gone back to Oral Roberts University after spending the summer with Jared. He and I saw each other most weekends. Either he would drive to Tulsa to see me, or I would drive to my parents' house in Yukon, and we would meet there. But this weekend was different. Hurricane Katrina had made landfall, wreaking havoc across many of the southern states just weeks prior, and struggling communities in that area needed a lot of help. One of the girls who lived on my floor in the dorm was from Louisiana, and her church back home was connected with an outreach providing disaster relief to displaced families. Her church gave our floor of girls and some of our guy friends who lived on the corresponding floor in the guys' dorm (called our brother wing) the opportunity to go and help in any way we could. So with very little planning, we got in our cars and drove to Louisiana one weekend.

One of the first nights after we had arrived, Jared called to check in. It was a phone call like any other. He told me about his day, and I told him about mine. We were best friends, but I believed that we would be nothing more, even though I was in love with him. He still planned to become a police officer, and my heart was set on professional ministry. I believed that if I was going to be in ministry with my husband, our hearts should be called toward the same thing. I was also eighteen, and my idea of what God wanted for my life wasn't very flexible.

I was just about to hang up the phone and join my friends, who were talking outside around the fire pit, when Jared said something funny, and it made me laugh. To this day, Jared is one of the few people I know who can consistently make me laugh in the middle of an ordinary conversation. I love that about him. Apparently, I have loved that about him from the beginning. Because while I can't remember exactly what he said, I know my response was laughter, followed by, "I love you."

And all at once I realized what I had done. I had told Jared that I loved him. It was out there. I couldn't take it back, and he and I both knew that I meant it. And we both knew *how* I had meant it. I hadn't said it as a friend says it to another friend. It was a profession of deep emotion. It was like a sigh. Something you can't control. Like my heart just had to breathe out those words. *I love you.*

I am sure it is no surprise to you that I remained completely collected and handled the situation calmly. Except I didn't. Until I take my very last breath, I will stand by my story that I actually threw the phone down and walked outside as if it hadn't happened. I hadn't even ended the call first. I had simply thrown the phone and then walked the other way. I found my friend, grabbed her, and shook her, shouting, "Do you know what I just did?! I just told Jared that I love him! I didn't mean to do that! I didn't even know I felt that way! What do I do now?!"

It took me a minute to clarify that Jared was probably still on the phone—in the kitchen—waiting to see if I was alive since I had abandoned our call five minutes earlier. She's a good friend, so she encouraged me to go back and talk to him and act as if nothing had happened. So that's exactly what I did. I walked back into the kitchen. I found my phone, and Jared hadn't hung up! It had been at least seven minutes since I had thrown down the phone in a panic, and he was still on the line saying, "Hello?" and asking me what had happened. He knew. And I knew. But he didn't push me to talk about it. I told him that I would call him later that weekend when I found a few free minutes but that we would probably be pretty busy doing what we had come to do.

For the next few days, that phone call and its implications consumed my thoughts. *Is this really how I feel about Jared? What am I supposed to do with these emotions? Is this what God would want for me? How did I let my heart get to this place? Why did I allow our relationship to continue like this if we aren't supposed to be together? And how can we go back to being friends when I am madly in love with this man?*

Fortunately, I stayed busy, and I didn't find a chance to talk to him before we headed home. On the drive I was in a crowded car, which made talking privately about what had happened impossible. By the time Jared and I were able to have a real conversation many days later, enough time had passed that we were able to act as if nothing had happened.

You obviously know the end of the story. God changed my heart and clarified His plan. Less than a month after the first time I told Jared, by accident, that I loved him, he said it back, on purpose. I remember the butterflies I felt in both moments. I remember realizing that my life would be completely different because I didn't just like this guy. I loved him.

Do you remember the first time you told your husband you loved him or the first time he told you? Do you remember where you were? Do you remember how it felt? Sometimes those early details of our relationships can get hazy. But I bet you remember how it felt to know you were loved, truly loved, by your husband in the beginning. There is something powerful about the words "I love you" that can change any regular conversation into something much, much more.

But I think you might agree that those words aren't always as powerful today as they were in the beginning. It could be they aren't as new or as fresh as they were in those first days. They are preserved with life and with familiarity as if canned or packaged. And while we may mean them, and we may say them more frequently today, I think we say them more flippantly sometimes.

I tell my husband I love him at the end of every phone call, because I want them to be the last words he hears me say should any tragedy keep me from saying another word to him. I do the same thing as he walks out of the house each morning. It is our standard close of conversation: "I love you. Bye." But as I began thinking what it would mean to live each day as if it were the first day that we fell in love, I realized there would be more excitement and power in the words "I love you." They wouldn't be packaged and airtight to have a long shelf life, like a bag of Goldfish crackers from the grocery store. They would be fresh and crisp and alive.

You can hear this freshness in my dad's "I love you." There is nothing stale about his words. As a matter of fact, if you happened to hear my dad telling my mom that he loves her, you might think he was saying those words to her for the first time. There is a passion and a promise that are understood and felt as he speaks those words directly into her heart. I don't think I have ever heard him say "I love you" without looking into her eyes. He doesn't say the words over his shoulder or as he's closing the front door to leave for work. He pauses, looks at her, and reminds her that those words are his truth.

So what about us? How do we put our hearts into the words we share with our husbands?

TODAY'S CHALLENGE

If today were the first day you fell in love with your husband, you would say "I love you" with passion. You would think about the power of those words. You wouldn't let them just fall from your lips. They would come from the depths of your heart. As we continue this journey into rediscovering our marriages in the midst of motherhood, I want you to consider the power of the words "I love you." Every time you say them today, I want you to think about how you felt the first time you said them to your husband. We aren't aiming to re-create the butterflies, but we are working to remind our hearts that our love for our husbands isn't just habit. It is a choice. It is the decision to profess with our mouths and believe with our hearts that we are saying yes to loving our husbands.

The times I most often say "I love you" to my husband absent-mindedly are . . .

_____

_____

_____

_____

_____

_____

_____

_____

_____

TALKING TO THE FATHER

Father God, thank You for reminding me of my love for my husband. It is so easy to be distracted by everything happening around me. Right now, Lord, I ask You to keep my words fresh. Don't let my "I love yous" go stale. As I continue this journey of looking back while moving forward, I ask that You would give a fresh outpouring of love on my husband and me. God, I love You. But sometimes my love for my husband is a little like my love for You. In the beginning I felt so passionately about You, and I wanted to profess my love and tell everyone I knew about how awesome you are. Lord, don't let my heart get to the place where loving You is routine. And if I am already there, rekindle the fire within me to love You and to show You that I love You with the same fervency I displayed in the beginning. I pray the same for my husband. Fan his love for You. Thank You, Lord, for who You are. Thank You for what You're doing now and what You've already done in my life. I love You, God. In the name of Jesus, I pray. Amen.

REFLECT

Did you notice a difference in your heart when you said "I love you" today? Did it remind you of how you felt when you said it the first time? Take a minute to write out the story of the first time you and your husband exchanged those words.

The first time my husband and I said, "I love you" to each other was . . .

_____

_____

_____

_____

_____

_____

_____

_____

Before we finish the day, I was wondering, What part of this process has been the hardest so far? What was the easiest? How does today rank from hardest to easiest?

_____

_____

_____

Discover Daily

Can you solve the mysteries of God?
Can you discover everything about the
Almighty?

— Job 11:7

I used to watch a popular reality TV show called *The Bachelor* and might still watch today if for some unknown reason the remote suddenly gets stuck on ABC on Monday night at seven. The premise of the show is simple. One guy gets to date more than two dozen women at the same time, and each week he eliminates women he doesn't feel a connection with until only one contestant remains. The aim of the show is for the bachelor to find a woman to marry as he gets to know each of the women through group and one-on-one settings.

A few weeks ago a new season of *The Bachelor* began, and my remote did that thing it does sometimes. As I was forced to watch this series with a bowl of popcorn and my favorite carbonated drink, I noticed that the bachelor this season told each of the women (in the limited time they had to talk alone), "I just can't wait to get to know you more" or "I'm looking forward to finding out who you are." Over and over he looked into the eyes of these women and in essence said, "I am interested in you, and I want to find out what makes you, you."

Because of the nature of the show, the contestants have a limited amount of time to fall in love, and they seem to make the most of it. They seem to realize that what it takes to fall in love is not only chemistry but something within their hearts that says, "I like who you are." Just a few dates into the season, the women began to share with this man their hopes and dreams, greatest fears and hurts, and childhood experiences, all while trying to win his heart by giving him a picture of who they are, where they come from, and what they are all about. As I watched this man decide what he liked and didn't like about each of them, I thought about how this principle translates into reality (not to be confused with reality TV).

When I first noticed Jared, I was curious about who he was. He wasn't just handsome. There was something about him that made me want to find out his story. Where was he from? What did he want to become? Who was the guy behind the curious smile? I liked the little bit I knew from our brief interactions, but the first time we went to dinner, I realized I had him all wrong.

First, Jared drove up to the restaurant in a giant burnt-orange, brand-new Chevy pickup. It was clean and well cared for and not at all what I was expecting. I thought he would drive a small, fast sports car. Most of the guys I had dated drove sports cars, and for some reason I thought he would be just like them. I had never dated a guy who drove a truck. I had never really been interested in a guy who drove a truck. Immediately I realized that Jared wasn't going to be like all the other guys I had gone out with. Not because of what he drove, but because he made different choices. He chose a truck while they chose cars, and I was genuinely interested in what else separated him from the others.

It was fun getting to know him, just as it was fun for him to get to know me. I think that is one of the most exciting parts of falling for someone—having a person say to you, "I like who you are. I want to know you better." It is the reason couples stay on the phone until three in the morning. It is the reason they text each other all day. It is the reason they spend hours upon hours together. They are learning about each other, and each new discovery makes them want to find out more, as if the relationship were like reading a good book they can't put down.

But at some point the newness wears off. It just does. It's not anyone's fault. We just know most of what there is to know. That's not falling in love. It's being in love. In my opinion, when a person knows most of what there is to know about someone else and chooses to continue an intimate relationship with that person, that's one facet of true love.

But when we think we know all there is to know about another person, we are essentially declaring that person will always be this way. It's as though we forget that the other person changes a little with each passing day, just as we do.

I realized this a couple of years ago when, eight years into our marriage, my husband suddenly took up bicycling. He bought this expensive bicycle and indoor bike trainer and these awesome bicycling clothes and signed up to ride seventy-five miles in a group ride.

Just when I thought I knew all there was to know about Jared Thompson, he became this bicyclist. And he really enjoyed it! But I did not see it coming. I had no idea he was even interested in bicycling.

But that's the thing. He might not have been even slightly interested in cycling when we first met. He might not have been interested five years into our marriage. But the day he became interested and decided to pursue it, I had two options. I could support him in exploring something new, or I could stand back and say, "Who are you? I don't even know you anymore."

The bicycling is a pronounced example of something I think most of us do every day without even realizing it. We don't refuse to let our husbands change, but rarely do we treat them as though there might be something about them we have yet to learn. Typically we believe we know all there is to know.

What if we asked our husbands about the dreams they still have in their hearts? What if we had conversations as though we were still interested in who they are becoming? What if we kept trying to get to know them?

The reality is, we might learn something brand-new. We might experience the joy of getting to know our husbands on another level. And our husbands would know they are free to keep discovering who they are. There is something powerful about a wife who can look into the heart of her husband and recognize the potential for new dreams. There is something empowering about giving our husbands permission to grow.

Today let's try looking at our husbands with fresh eyes. Rediscovering our marriages isn't just about what we do; it is also about shifting how we think. So let's try this. I understand that most of the mystery behind the man you sleep with each night is gone. But when was the last time you thought about the dreams in his heart? When was the last time you asked him about them? When was the last time you looked at him as though you might discover something new if you asked the right questions? How would you listen to him if you thought he might tell you something you didn't already know?

Today's Challenge

For today's challenge we are going to have a simple conversation with our husbands. If today were the first day you fell in love, you would ask questions that prompted the answers you were the most curious about. Here are today's conversation starters: How does your husband feel about his job? How does he feel about his family? How does he feel about your relationship? Consider using these prompts the next time you two have a few minutes alone or even during dinner with your family. Your children could benefit from learning more about their father. Even if the concepts are a bit over their heads, they should see their parents having healthy conversations.

Finally, the next chance you get, ask your husband this question: "What's one thing about you I don't already know?" Then tell him one thing about you. It's not about the answers, friend. It is about the attitude of the heart that asks. Give him grace to grow, and take the time to keep discovering him. Because getting to know him should take a lifetime.

Here are the questions I am going to ask him . . .

_____

_____

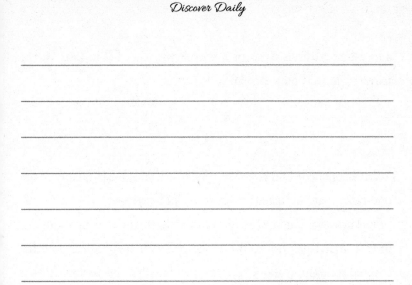

TALKING TO THE FATHER

Lord, I thank You for being a God who never changes. You are the same yesterday, today, and forever. But, Lord, my husband and I are always changing, always growing. We are always learning what it means to follow You and love each other as You have asked. I am on a journey of discovering who I am in You, and when I married, my husband's journey and my journey overlapped. They intertwine now. God, at times our hearts become tangled, and we stop letting each other grow. Lord, don't let us hold each other back. Don't let us set up barriers that keep us from becoming who You have called us to be. But as we allow each other to grow, help my husband and me choose to get to know each other in new ways, to explore the places within our hearts that we don't often speak of, and to walk in a love that reminds us of how we felt when we fell in love. In the name of Jesus, I pray. Amen.

REFLECT

What happened? Did you take time to ask your husband any of the questions that you listed? If so, how did he answer? Were you surprised by anything he said? Have there been any specific moments in your marriage prior to this when you were surprised as you discovered something about your spouse? Finally, why do you think it is important to allow our husbands to continue growing?

Here's how it went . . .

_____

_____

_____

_____

_____

_____

_____

Day 20

Love Unexpectedly

Three things will last forever—faith, hope,
and love—and the greatest of these is love.

—1 Corinthians 13:13

J ared and I had spent only a little bit of time getting to
know each other when I found myself thinking about him
while I waited to order a snow cone. As I was sitting in the drive-
through line, I wondered what flavor Jared might like. He had quit
his job at the mall and was working at a nearby golf course. Knowing he was at work, I sent him a quick text message: "What is your
favorite snow cone flavor?" I thought I would drop in and take him
a treat. Since I didn't get to see him every day anymore, I took every
chance I could to spend time with him.

My phone buzzed, and I flipped it open. He had replied with

two words: "Surprise me." I didn't know him well at this point, so it felt more like a test than a treat, but I had a plan.

The car in front of me pulled away, and I drove up to the window. I gave them my order and then told them I also wanted one regular-sized snow cone in their most popular flavor. I paid, and they handed me my cherry-flavored frozen treat and one Purple Rain. It looked . . . interesting, but it was delicious! (I knew Jared well enough to steal a bite of the surprise I had paid for.)

Less than ten minutes later, I was in the parking lot where Jared worked, and I sent a text: "I've got something for you. Can you come outside?" He was sweaty from working, but I liked the guy so much it didn't even faze me. I hugged him and handed him his purple snow cone. Just because.

And just like that, I had gone out of my way to make his day a little better without much effort or planning.

Do you remember the simple little things you did for your husband when you first fell in love with him? I'm not talking about elaborate displays of affection. I'm talking about sweet, simple details that told the story of how much you cared about him.

If we're both honest, we have probably forgotten many of the simple things we did, because at the time they didn't seem memorable. They just came naturally. Of course, some of them stand out, but I bet there are dozens more, and if we could go back and replay the tapes we would say, "Oh! I didn't even remember doing that for him."

I think this is one of the areas of a mature marriage that is the least like new love. We just aren't as considerate of our husbands today. It isn't that we are being rude. It is that our attention level has dropped from its peak in the beginning. Back then I didn't get a drink for myself without offering one to Jared as well. I didn't skip one opportunity to surprise him or show him I was thinking about him, and I was always thinking about him.

The reality is that the demand for our attention today has reduced the amount of time we have to think about our husbands. When I run to the grocery store with my three young children, I'm just trying to avoid all forms of a meltdown, and the last thing on my mind is what sort of candy bar Jared might want as a snack later in the day. When I'm getting my kids to and from school and all their extracurricular activities, I don't generally think, *Does Jared need me to drive to his office and bring him a cookie?*

It's not that I don't love him. It is simply that I'm preoccupied.

Of course, if this were the first day we fell in love, we wouldn't have to work to find the time. It would just come naturally. But that aspect of this challenge might not be possible. Hardly any part of the process of rediscovering our marriage is an easy, natural response, because time has stolen the newness. But, friend, you did all those simple, wonderful things in the beginning because you wanted your husband to know you were thinking about him. You wanted him to feel loved, and in turn, loving him made you feel good too.

My dad has made a habit of surprising my mom with turtles—figurine turtles, in case you were wondering. My mom began collecting these tiny glass turtles a couple of years ago, so my dad bought a few when my mom wasn't with him. He would leave them in different places around the house to surprise her. Once he placed a porcelain turtle on her teacup saucer. Another time he left one next to her toothbrush holder. She never knew where a turtle would pop up next. These little surprises didn't require a lot of thought, but they told her that my dad was thinking about her and wanted her to feel loved. And while there are many kinds of surprises, the ones that say someone wants us to feel special are the best kind.

So my question for you is this: Do you continue to show your husband in unexpected ways that you still love him?

TODAY'S CHALLENGE

Today isn't just about doing one thing for your husband. We've already discussed how much you do for him, and we've already taken a step to refocus our hearts as we do those things for our husbands. Today I want us to surprise them. It doesn't have to be an elaborate gift. Money and its importance are an entirely separate issue of married life. But I want you to think of something you could do for your husband to love him in a way he won't expect. Ideas? You could drop a cup of coffee off at his office or put a note in his briefcase or lunchbox. You could make sure you have his favorite snack or bake him something just because. What are a few things you might do for your husband?

I'm going to surprise him by . . .

_____

_____

_____

_____

_____

_____

_____

_____

As I love my husband unexpectedly now, I get excited with the joy of giving. Even when I was younger, I always wanted to give presents to my family early because I couldn't wait to see their reaction. I feel the same way now as I do these simple things for Jared. But his reaction isn't the point. He may not gush about how amazing I am the way he did when we first fell in love. But what matters is that I am retraining my heart to look for ways to love him unexpectedly, and I am reestablishing the simple things as an active part of our married love.

TALKING TO THE FATHER

Lord, it's easy to fall into a routine and let distraction dictate how I show my love for my husband. But, God, I pray now that You will help me find ways to love him unexpectedly. Help me remember him throughout my day. Put him on my heart while I'm in the middle of everything else that occupies my time and my thoughts. Continue to fan the flame of fresh love in my heart and in my husband's heart so the simple things again become a vital part of how we demonstrate our continued affection for each other. Lord, I remember that each small gesture is a significant seed I am planting in my marriage. Help me never to miss one chance to show him just how much I love him. Finally, God, I ask that You would place excitement in my heart as I think of fun new ways to be my husband's best friend. In the name of Jesus, I pray. Amen.

REFLECT

So what did you do? And how did you feel? What was your husband's response? Is this something you would consider continuing? Why?

Here's how it went . . .

_____

_____

_____

_____

_____

_____

_____

_____

_____

_____

_____

_____

_____

_____

_____

One thing I want to make sure to do as we near the end of the challenge is give you the opportunity to note anything worth remembering about this process. What is happening in your marriage right now that you're surprised by, hopeful for, praying about, looking forward to?

_____

_____

_____

_____

_____

_____

_____

_____

_____

_____

_____

_____

Day 21

Interact Patiently

Love is patient, love is kind. It does not envy,
it does not boast, it is not proud. It does not
dishonor others, it is not self-seeking, it is not
easily angered, it keeps no record of wrongs.
Love does not delight in evil but rejoices with
the truth. It always protects, always trusts,
always hopes, always perseveres. Love never
fails.

1 Corinthians 13:4–8, NIV

There are a pair of work jeans and white socks on our bathroom floor where my husband left them when he got home
from work and changed his clothes. This is the case at our house
most days. No matter how close he is to the laundry basket, no matter how many times I remind him, no matter how much I thank

him for picking up his laundry when he remembers to do it, many days I still walk into the bathroom and find his clothes on the floor.

In the beginning of our marriage, I thought this was kinda cute. *Oh, look! He didn't put away his work clothes. I'll do it!* It was a little annoying because I had asked him to do it, but I wasn't upset. It was part of that time in our relationship when it was fun to do those simple things for him. Fast-forward ten years, and when I walk into the bathroom and find his jeans on the floor, I have to count backward from ten, reminding myself they are just dirty clothes and he had a long day.

Please tell me there is something about your husband that requires you to demonstrate patience too. I'm sure there is. In fact, I'm sure there are plenty of things about your husband that you thought were so cute in the beginning. *Yes, he bites his nails, but don't a lot of guys? He might trim his toenails in our bed, but at least he collects the pieces. He doesn't always put the toilet seat down, but he won't do that forever.* But years or even months later you find yourself thinking, *Will he ever quit!?*

Dear newlywed self,

Grace, sister. Stock up on grace and patience so you
will never run out of either. You will need a lifetime supply.

Do you ever feel this way? Do you ever think about all the adorable, quirky things your husband did when you first fell in love that make you feel a little batty today? Let's be honest for a second. We've been pretty good about being honest throughout this journey. Love is patient, but sometimes we are not. We want patience for ourselves. We understand the importance of patience. But oftentimes we have a hard time being patient with others. Or is it just me?

Sometimes I'm in too much of a hurry to be patient. But that's not how the Lord would have me love or engage with my husband. God is endlessly patient with me, and He asks that I show the same type of patience with my husband.

I guess I'm guilty of thinking that if my husband would just quit doing that really annoying thing—whatever it happens to be—then I wouldn't need to be patient with him. But I don't need Jared to stop doing all those things that drive me nuts. (I would like it, but it's not what I really need.) I need to stop feeling the way I do when he does those things. Because when I really think about it, Jared has done most of the stuff that drives me crazy, well, forever. What has changed is how I look at him and how I feel about what I consider to be his less-than-ideal qualities.

You see, patience isn't just diffusing the anger before we explode or making the choice not to lash out when we are upset. Patience is what keeps us from getting angry in the first place. It is the filter through which all other aspects of love flow into a relationship. I think the reason that Scripture begins with patience in the long list of love's attributes is because if we don't have patience, we can't have any of the rest of love. Patience allows us to be kind. It allows us to experience joy by separating us from frustration. It helps us avoid keeping a record of wrongs. The list goes on. Patience isn't just something we do; it is something we are. And if we are going to show love to our husbands, we have to figure out how to be more patient.

In previous chapters we talked a little about having grace for the fathers our husbands have become. We talked about allowing our husbands to continue to grow into the men God is calling them to be. But, friend, how you interact with the man right in front of you today requires the grace that only patience can provide. Because when we have patience, we are able to love our husbands just as they are without requiring them to change first.

So what do we do? How do we have patience for our husbands when we have to be patient all day with everyone else? How do we keep pouring out what everyone needs from us?

If today were the first day you were married to your husband, no one would have to tell you to give him a second chance. No one would have to tell you not to become upset when he did that one annoying thing, because you probably wouldn't find it annoying. The grace for your husband would still be fresh and in good supply.

Scripture calls patience one of the fruit of the Spirit. And fruit isn't created by our hands; it is produced by a tree. Friend, when our lives are not producing the fruit we want to see, it is important that we examine where our lives are planted. Are you planted in the good ground of God's love and His Word? Are you spending time with the Lord in prayer or worship?

I wish I had a formula so you could create more patience on your own, but if you want to grow more patience in your marriage, you need to address the ground surrounding your heart. You need to see where you're planted.

TODAY'S CHALLENGE

Today's challenge might take all day. It might take all year. It might take the rest of our lives. We are going to show patience to our husbands as if it were the first day we fell in love. Does he need you to repeat something one more time? Okay. No sighing. Did he leave his dirty clothes next to the hamper and the cap off the toothpaste? It's okay. Do you feel like arguing? You're going to breathe through it instead. Perfect. Patience is about more than not losing your temper. It is about a million opportunities to share love. And the beautiful thing about each opportunity to extend grace and show your patience is that you're planting seeds of love that will bear fruit later.

What are some things about your husband that drive you crazy? Knowing these areas where you lack patience can prepare your heart to demonstrate it later.

Day 21

Here's where I need to demonstrate patience . . .

_____

_____

_____

_____

_____

_____

_____

_____

Do you think today's challenge to be continually patient with your husband is going to be easy or hard? Explain.

I think being continually patient is going to be . . .

_____

_____

_____

_____

_____

_____

_____

_____

_____

_____

Talking to the Father

Lord, thank You for Your continued patience with me. Thank You for not losing Your temper or being an angry God. Thank You for giving me as many chances as I need to get something right. That includes showing my husband patience, Lord. Thank You for giving me the chance to be patient with him. I ask that every time I show my husband patience, I would remember that You demonstrate the same kind of love toward me. Let each of those moments be gifts when I can remember Your kindness toward me. And help me look to You as the source of my strength as I pour out endless love from the good ground of my heart. This process of rediscovering how to love my husband isn't always an easy one, but I'm learning that all marriages need patience in order to grow. Help me be patient as I complete this process. In the name of Jesus, I pray. Amen.

Reflect

So how did it go? How do you feel about today's challenge? Did you notice a difference in how your husband responded to you when you acted patiently?

Here's how it went . . .

_____

_____

_____

_____

_____

_____

_____

_____

I cannot think of a better challenge to end our journey. We won't just need to repeat this tomorrow; we will need to repeat this every day forever. We will need to be patient not only with our husbands but with ourselves as well. We will need to remember that this process of rediscovering our marriages takes time. We will need to be patient as we continue to walk each day in intentional love.

Take a minute to think back over the last twenty-one days. What did you take away from this process? What are you hoping to continue? What did you realize you already do well? And what are you looking forward to in the future as you journey toward love unending?

_____

_____

_____

_____

_____

_____

_____

Conclusion

Before We End

My dad leaned back in his chair and said, "So what do you think? Could you do it? It's possible. I haven't been successful every day. I'm human. But I've tried every day. Just as I strive to know and love the Lord with a new love every day, I want to show your mom the same type of covenant love. I did this on my own without expecting anything in return. Without your mom even knowing I was intentionally showing her love in this way. Because at the end of the day, I want to be the person who loves her like Jesus. That's the type of love I want to show your mom. That's the type of love you can give too. It's work, and it's hard, but at the end of the day, it's always worth it. Tomorrow you'll be glad you did it. What do you think? Could you do it? It's possible. I know because I lived it."

And now you and I have discovered the same truths my dad spoke about that night. We know for ourselves that it is possible to experience this type of love. We know that it isn't always easy. We know that some days we won't *want* to do it. We know that some days we won't do it. But we know the changes that can take place in our hearts when we try. We know the power of a clean slate every morning and an intentional way to show love each day. We might not have lived this way for nearly forty years like my dad, but we are now well on our journey toward living a Love Unending.

Let's pray before you go.

Lord, if I learned anything over the last twenty-one days, it is that there are so many opportunities for me to show my husband that I love him. There are so many aspects to our marriage that have the possibility to change over time, but there is something so powerful about going back to the beginning and starting fresh right where we are. That's my prayer for myself and for my friend reading these words. I pray that every day we would remember the power of a clean slate. I pray that we would remember the hope in a new tomorrow. And I pray that we would remember the promise of love unending.

I pray for every marriage impacted by these words, Lord. I pray that husbands and wives would turn toward each other and turn toward You. I pray that love would be reignited and relationships would be restored. Touch our families, Lord. Encourage every heart. And secure the truths we have gained as we continue to rediscover marriage in the midst of motherhood.

In the name of Jesus I pray. Amen.

Acknowledgments

To my parents, Marc and Susan Pitts: Thank you for living out the example of this journey. Thank you for showing me that marriage with an endless sort of love is possible. Thank you for realizing that the greatest gift parents can give their children is a secure marriage. Thank you for that gift in my life. Dad, your choice to follow the Lord as He asked you to love Mom in this way has allowed all of us to follow you. Every life affected by this book will be a result of your bravery and obedience to walk out the life and love that God revealed to you. Thank you for your faithfulness to the Lord, to Mom, and to our family.

To my husband, Jared: When we married young, we might not have known much about what to expect in a marriage, but we knew how we felt about forever. We knew we weren't entering into an experiment. We knew our love wasn't a trial run. It wasn't "Let's see if this works and then go from there." We understood that we were tying our hearts to each other, following the covenant that Jesus entered into with His people as our example. His love is unending, and my prayer is that we would fully understand and show each other that same kind of love every single day.

To my children, Kolton, Kadence, and Jaxton: I cannot promise to love your daddy perfectly. But I can promise that if you watch us and how we love each other, you will learn many lessons. You will learn how to give grace, how to make mistakes and ask for forgiveness, how to accept others as they are, and how to cheer them on as they become all they were meant to be. It is my prayer that your daddy and I can give you the same gift your nana and papa gave me. It is my prayer that you would witness firsthand love unending.

To my Scissortail SILK community: You all are the reason I wrote this book. Your comments and your responses every time I shared how I feel about balancing being a wife and a mom compelled me to look for answers. Because of you, I wanted to discover a way we could remember how to be wives in the middle of motherhood. Thank you for making our community such a beautiful and safe place to gather. Thank you for your open arms. Thank you for your encouraging words. Thank you for always reaching out to more women who need to find hope. May we use this book as a launching pad for a generation of women who want to love their husbands well.

Finally, none of what has been written here would be true without the love that Jesus first showed me. Scripture reminds us in 1 John 4:19, "We love, because He first loved us" (NASB). When I am tempted to say I don't want to love my husband or the world around me because they haven't shown love to me, I am reminded that true love isn't a response. It is an action. Thank You, Lord, for teaching me how to love first as I follow Your example.